WESTERN
ISLAMIC
ARCHITECTURE

WESTERN ISLAMIC ARCHITECTURE

A Concise Introduction
with 139 Illustrations

JOHN D. HOAG

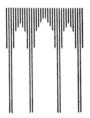

DOVER PUBLICATIONS, INC.
Mineola, New York

Bibliographical Note

This Dover edition, first published in 2005, is an unabridged republication of the work originally published in 1963 by George Braziller, New York, under the title *Western Islamic Architecture.*

Library of Congress Cataloging-in-Publication Data

Hoag, John D.
  Western Islamic architecture : a concise introduction / John D. Hoag.
    p. cm.
  Originally published: New York : G. Braziller, 1963.
  Includes bibliographical references and index.
  ISBN 0-486-43760-4 (pbk.)
    1. Architecture, Islamic—History. I. Title.

NA380.H63 2005
723'.3—dc22

2004056204

Manufactured in the United States of America
Dover Publications, Inc., 31 East 2nd Street, Mineola, N.Y. 11501

CONTENTS

INTRODUCTION
"In the name of the merciful and compassionate god"

Never in history has one people so rapidly come to rule half the known world as did the Arabs after the death of Muhammad in 632. Muhammad's creed, embodied in the Koran, is known as Islam—literally "resignation to the will of God." There are two dogmas. First, God is one; and in this all the sacramental elements of Christianity are denied. Second, Muhammad was the messenger of God, the last of a line of prophets including those of the Old Testament as well as Christ. When Muhammad redirected his prayers from the Temple at Jerusalem to the Kaaba at Mecca, the ancient Arabian center of pagan pilgrimage, he turned Islam into a national Arab movement.

Surah 35 of the Koran says, "And no burdened soul shall bear the burden of another... and he who is pure is only pure for himself and unto God the journey is." [1] And, Surah 7, "Every nation has its appointed time and when their appointed time comes they cannot keep it back an hour, nor can they bring it on." Such resignation to a preordained fate, coupled with the search for a purely personal salvation—more Buddhist than Semitic—grew as the Arab conquests moved eastward across Persia. This attitude encouraged the development of the autocrat, with the result that Muslim history has ever since been one of almost continuous political fragmentation. No dynasty maintained its power for much more than 200 years and few for that long. The persistent growth, despite these chaotic conditions, of a Muslim civilization whose architectural style is recognizable from Spain to India is a greater miracle even than the initial Arab military successes.

Islamic architectural invention concentrates around two major programs, the mosque and the palace. It is always in one or the other that the style gives clearest expression to its inner meanings; but even though forms borrowed from one may be used for the other, the two programs express fundamentally opposed concepts.

The mosque is a shelter and a refuge from the turbulent life of the crowded city. Each Friday the thousands its open *sahn*, or interior court, and its covered prayer hall may accommodate bow down in unison toward the *qibla* wall which faces Mecca. All over the world they turn toward the one center like so many iron filings attracted by a magnet. They are a mass and yet separate, each intent upon his own salvation, each wrapped in an inner calm unknown to a Westerner. "O ye who believe! enter ye into the peace, one and all," Surah 11 calls. The architectural setting sustains and enhances this mood, whether there be one worshiper or a multitude. The endless cadence of arch and column, articulating the continuous space into identical segments, by itself could bring about such a state, but the mood is also greatly enhanced by ornament. Like the architecture as a whole, Islamic ornament is totally nonsculptural. It does not impel to action but invites contemplation by the challenge of its infinite complexity. Polychromed or incised in very low relief, it proliferates with a kind of organic growth of its own. It encrusts the surfaces of walls, vaults, and piers, dematerializing them, yet never interfering with their major outlines. The interlace, infinitely varied, swallows everything, even the verses of the Koran, whose exquisite Kufic script becomes so ornate that only an expert can read it. Like the high pictured windows of a Gothic church, seen from the floor purely as a blaze of light, the inscriptions do not instruct, but surround. Their contemplation frees the surrendering mind, and their complexity triumphantly declares the infinite oneness of God.

The palace, on the other hand, employs every resource of architectural symbolism to emphasize the power and authority of the ruler. He is enthroned at the heart of an axial composition more intricate than any accorded a pagan idol or a Christian altar.

In the palace complexes those parts devoted to the private use of the ruler embodied another meaning. Throughout the Koran, when Muhammad speaks of paradise, he constantly uses the phrase, "Gardens beneath which rivers flow." Once he says, "For them are upper chambers and upper chambers above them built beneath which rivers flow." There the elect were to be clothed in green silk and to be entertained by large-eyed maidens beside the four rivers of paradise. In the Koran, the word firdaws is used several times for paradise. It comes from the Persian faradis, derived from a word meaning a place walled in, or the finest and highest part of a garden. In the lavish use of fountains, quadripartite courts, and pavilions overlooking basins of water, many Islamic palaces, in their private portions, seem deliberately intended by their builders to provide a setting for the anticipation upon earth of the pleasures of the hereafter.

The mosque and palace concepts just described affect nearly all other major programs of Islamic architecture. The madrasa, or theological school, borrows elements from both, while the *han*, or caravanserai, owes much to the palace. Even relatively modest private dwellings preserve in their ceremonial apartments certain elements from the palace plan; and their gardens, on a small scale, also anticipate paradise. To serve these chosen purposes, the Muslims adapted the architectural symbolism, structural methods, and ornament of various peoples they conquered. Once this amalgam became established, about 900 A.D., geographical isolation, the conversion of new peoples to Islam, and the sheer weight of centuries effected a number of variants within the style.

1 THE FORMATIVE YEARS

THE ORTHODOX CALIPHS (632–61)

Until they began their conquests, which by 661 had made them rulers of the areas now forming Palestine, Transjordan, Egypt, Syria, Iraq, and Iran, the Arabs were innocent of any architectural tradition. The Koran, Surah 7, says, "God... made for you, of the skins of cattle, houses that ye may find them light on the day ye move your quarters and the day when ye abide..." Muhammad is also quoted as having said, "The most unprofitable thing that eateth up the wealth of a believer is building." [2] The earliest congregational mosques for the Friday communal prayer were square enclosures surrounded by reeds or a ditch and oriented toward Mecca. Their essential equipment evolved slowly. The *minbar*, or pulpit (plate 30), was a raised chair first used by Muhammad at Medina so that crowds of the faithful could see and hear him. Its ascent by the caliphs who immediately succeeded him became part of their installation ceremony. Only after 750 did it become a pulpit used in all mosques.

The final conquest of the Sassanian Kingdom of Iraq and Persia was accomplished in 637 by Sa'd ibn al-Waqqas when he captured and sacked Ctesiphon, its capital. Sa'd, one of the

Prophet's favorite followers and the descendant of an aristocratic Meccan family, then founded Kufa on the western arm of the Euphrates, south of Babylon. There, on the orders of the Caliph, Omar, he built a governor's residence, Dar al-Imara, adjacent to the *qibla* wall of the mosque (plate 1). When the structure was described to Omar he was so incensed that upon Sa'd's dismissal in 640 he is even said to have ordered it burned.[3] Only the plan can be traced, but it is enough to explain why. A single north-south axis led through both enclosures to a court of honor with recessed porches or *iwans* in the center of each of its four sides. That to the south opened into a basilical hall terminated by a square, four-doored chamber, probably once domed. Sa'd had taken for himself all the royal symbolism of Sassanian kingship, and Omar was quite right in assuming that the symbol might soon become a reality. Sa'd retired from political life soon after; but temptation, aided by poor communication as the Empire expanded, was too much for many of his successors.

THE UMAYYAD CALIPHATE (661–750)

After the defeat and death of Ali; the last orthodox Caliph, Mu'awiyah, first of the Umayyads, moved the capital of the Empire from Medina to Damascus. The ascent of the Umayyads, marked a period of relative materialism for Islam. Fond of poetry and wine, the Umayyads were aristocrats who soon abolished election to their office, preferring to appoint their sons or brothers. It was under them that two more characteristic pieces of mosque furniture were developed. The first was a windowed wall of wood or brick which surrounded the *minbar* and the caliph's place of prayer. This was called the *maqsura*[4] (plate 86) and was introduced either by Mu'awiya in 664–65 or by Marwan in 683–85. In either case, the intent was to protect the caliph from attempts upon his life. The idea was soon taken up by the governors and spread from one end of Islam to the other. When, in 707–09, the Caliph al-Walid rebuilt the mosque at Medina, formerly Muhammad's house, he introduced a niche, the *mihrab*, in the center of the *qibla* wall (plate 56). Because the niche had obvious affiliations with Christian architecture, it was at first opposed by the orthodox but, nevertheless, soon became universal. The *mihrab* is purely a directional symbol, and there may be more than one in any mosque. Nevertheless, the central *mihrab*, like an apse, gave even the earliest congregational mosques a strong axial emphasis.

11

The earliest surviving architectural masterpiece built under Islam is the Dome of the Rock, begun probably in 688–89 and completed, according to its dated inscription, in 691–92 by the Caliph Abd al-Malik. It stands in the Haram as Sharif (plates 2, 4), a great rectangular enclosure in an area of Jerusalem once occupied by the Jewish Temple but never built upon by the Christians. Near its center is the *sakhra*, the bare rock surface of the summit of Mt. Moriah, one of the most ancient sacred sites in the world and the traditional place of Abraham's sacrifice. Here, Abd-al-Malik built not a mosque in the tradition set by Muhammad's house at Medina, but a ciborium like a Christian martyrium.

The exterior walls are sheathed in quartered marble to the window line. Above, where there are now Turkish tiles installed in 1554, there were once glass mosaics which covered the drum of the great wooden dome as well. The dome, a twelfth-century replacement of the original, was probably, then as now, gilded. In the white Palestinian sunlight the structure glows like a jeweled reliquary. Four portals lead from the four cardinal directions into the first ambulatory where the dominant direction is horizontal, stressed by the very Roman combination of an entablature under arches. Beyond the inner octagon, space opens and one faces four, rather than three, arches unobstructed by entablatures (plate 6). Finally, the great upward thrust of the space beneath the dome enhances the sanctity of the site it protects. The geometric order of plan and elevation (plate 3) produces a satisfying sensation of harmony, aided by the luxury of the rich polychrome ornament of marble, hammered bronze, and mosaic. This is not an Arab building, but neither is it entirely Byzantine; the ambiguity may have been intentional.

The Arabs claimed descent from Abraham. Abd al-Malik's rival, the Caliph Ibn al-Zubayr who ruled at Mecca from 683 to 692, is said to have rebuilt the Kaaba as the Prophet had said it was in the time of Abraham. This was accomplished in 684, and the structure was ornamented with mosaics from a church in the Yemen. According to an early tradition, Abd al-Malik intended the Dome of the Rock to function as a rival Kaaba in order to transfer the *hajj* or pilgrimage from Mecca to Jerusalem, placing it on the site of Muhammad's ascent to Heaven. It has recently been pointed out[5] that Muhammad's ascent is commemorated elsewhere on the Haram, and that Abd al-Malik, in fact, wished to recall the sacrifice of Abraham. The building itself echoes the Holy Sepulcher in the rhythm of its inner arcade (plate 5). Possibly, the Dome of the Rock was to have been a victory monument reflecting the theological and political situation of its own time and the hopes of Islam to gather to itself the two faiths which had preceded it.[6]

When Damascus was taken in 635 the Muslims shared the temenos of the temple of Jupiter with the Christians, whose Church of St. John probably occupied the site of the temple proper. In 705 the Caliph al-Walid (705–15) purchased the church and destroyed it. He used the space of the temenos for his new Congregational Mosque, begun in 706 and finished in 714/15 (plate 7). On the south (in Syria almost exactly oriented toward Mecca) he built three aisles divided in the center by a transverse nave lighted by a clerestory and provided with a dome, originally wooden, over the center bay. Single *riwaqs*, or arcades, were also added to the north, west, and east sides of the temenos. The four ancient corner towers became minarets, the first in Islam. Finally, above the alternate columns and piers of the arcades and above a zone of quartered marble paneling around the walls of the temenos, were added a superb series of decorative mosaics (plate 8). The floral and architectural compositions with their mixture of formal oriental tradition and Hellenistic illusionism point here as in Jerusalem to a local Syrian tradition.

The mosque at Damascus is the earliest surviving example of the complete assimilation by the Muslims of foreign architectural elements and their new use of them to establish an environment specifically their own. The great court recalls Muhammad's house at Medina, but the rhythm of the surrounding arcades, where piers alternate with paired columns (plate 9), repeats that of the now-vanished atrium of Hagia Sophia at Constantinople. The central gable of the *mihrab* transept (plate 10) may echo a palace façade like that of the Chalki at Constantinople. Like the dome over the same transept, long a royal symbol, the architecture may here also have been intended to enhance the position of the Caliph as sovereign.

The Umayyad caliphs were, and remained, desert Arabs with nomadic habits. Self-indulgent and pleasure loving, they spent most of their time away from Damascus in semipermanent camps, or *badiyas*, where they maintained gardens and walled hunting preserves. In both the irrigation of their gardens and the use of game preserves they had probably adapted methods from the Sassanians before them. However, the bathing establishments which formed essential parts of such sites were based on late Roman models surely available then in Syria. Qusayr Amra, about 50 miles east of Amman in Transjordan, was built about 715 (plates 11, 12). It consisted only of a bath and an attached audience hall, once sumptuously ornamented with mosaics, marble, and frescoes. The proprietor's followers must have camped in tents. At Qasr al-Kharanah, not far away, a two-story residence is well preserved. It is dated only by an Arabic graffito of 711 in one of the upper rooms, but was probably built not long before.

The almost windowless enclosure is entered from the south through a split semicircular tower (plate 14). Two stairways give access to the upper floor symmetrically disposed about an open court (plate 13). To judge from its rich ornament, this was the *piano nobile* and, of its rooms, the most important is a formerly domed reception room with the only window in the building overlooking the entrance. The rest of this floor consists of a series of independent apartments for retainers or wives, and several more occupy the ground floor. These are called *bayts*, Arabic for house, and are of a type found only in Syria, Transjordan, or Palestine; never in Iraq. On the other hand, the rubble masonry—using liberal amounts of mortar—and the stilted, round arched windows suggest that the builders had a Sassanian background. Possibly also Sassanian is the presence of the domed chamber over the entrance. If the Umayyads did not practice the elaborate gate ceremonial of the later Abbasids they had at least already adapted an architecture appropriate to such ceremonies.

Khirbet al-Mafjar, in the Jordan Valley, was perhaps already under construction in 743–44. However, only the bath was complete and in use when the whole was destroyed, probably by an earthquake, in 747–48. The complex included a walled irrigated tract of about 150 acres. The immediate surroundings of the mansion consist of a roughly rectangular enclosure (plate 15), bounded on the east by the house itself; a mosque; and a very elaborate bathing establishment.

The bath is the most monumental of all such Umayyad structures. The entrance porch can be restored with fair accuracy from the remnants of its stucco and stone ornament (plate 19). A very complex system of borrowing and adaptation had clearly been going on, accompanied by a well-developed *horror vacui* and an interest in flat surface patterns in shallow relief which did not interfere with the simple massive form of the gate. The composition suggests a Roman triumphal arch; but the crenelations, dome, and statue of a caliph in the niche are all of Sassanian origin. The great hall of the bath supported an elaborate system of barrel vaults, clerestories, and domes on compound piers of stone, the whole rising from a mosaic floor of local Palestinian type. The curvilinear knots and interlaces of this mosaic (plate 16) became an inseparable part of Islamic architectural ornament. At the northeast corner was a room which must have served as a private audience chamber. A bench lined three walls, while the fourth was occupied by a deep niche with a raised mosaic floor. A reconstruction based on the fallen stucco ornament (plate 18) shows the sumptuous eclecticism which prevailed everywhere. The winged horses in the *tondi* set in the pendentives of the dome are Sassanian royal emblems. Western and oriental elements are combined, indicating the progress already made toward the creation of a new style.

Of the mansion, only the ground floor is preserved; but fragments fallen from above show that the state apartments, as at Qasr al-Kharanah, stood above the main entrance, where they surrounded a dome chamber which had a window of appearances in which the ruler could appear before his subjects (plate 17). The house was closely linked to its walled garden through a two-story portico with compound piers below. The domed pavilion over the garden pool, the richness of the ornament, the elaborate provisions for the reception of visitors, and the repeated use of architectural symbolism associated with kingship suggest that the owner was a very important person.[7]

Possibly the last and certainly the most ambitious of all the Umayyad country seats was the unfinished palace of Mshatta whose construction was probably interrupted by the fall of the dynasty in 750. The palace stands about twenty miles south of Amman on the border between the ancient provinces of Syria and Iraq. The material is well-cut stone which is characteristically Syrian; but the brick vaults are more typical of Iraq, as is the plan (plate 21). An enclosure about 480 feet square is divided on the north-south axis as at Kufa into three parts. The center part, like Kufa, consists of an antechamber, court of honor, and basilical throne hall. The triconch throne room proper, probably adapted from a Syrian example (the Audience Hall of the episcopal palace at Bosra), was closely linked both in Rome and Byzantium with imperial architectural symbolism.[8] The four *bayts* are also of Syrian plan, recalling Qasr al-Kharanah and Khirbet al-Mafjar. The wonderful carvings of the south façade, now in the Berlin Museum (plate 20), combine the six-lobed rosettes and octagons of Khirbet al-Mafjar with triangular "pediments" framed in continuous moldings. Persian and Hellenistic elements are inextricably blended in the deeply undercut sculpture, producing a flickering play of light and dark over the amber-colored sandstone.

THE EARLY ABBASID CALIPHATE (750–892)

The Abbasids overthrew the last Umayyad Caliph with the assistance of Persian soldiers and cavalry, thereby introducing a new wave of influence from the East. The second Caliph, al-Mansur (754–75), founded a new capital at Baghdad in 762. Nothing remains of this capital, but we know from contemporary descriptions that it was circular with four equidistant gates. In the center of an inner enclosure was the palace and a mosque. The palace was called either the Green Dome or the Golden Gate, after its principal components. We are told that the green dome stood at the end of an *iwan*, thus repeating the arrangement at Kufa. Probably the gate, which had its own dome of gold, was on axis with the *iwan*, also as at Kufa. The increased emphasis on the entrance is closely related to the more elaborate gate ceremonial adopted by the Abbasids, who revived the ancient custom of appearing before their subjects at a window above the main entrance of a palace, called the window of appearances.[9]

Ukhaidir, a fortified country palace about 75 miles southwest of Baghdad, has a plan (plate 22) strikingly like Kufa's. It was probably built after 774–75 by Isa Ibn Musa, a nephew of the Caliph al-Mansur and the only important member of the Abbasid family known to have lived in exile.[10] The outer enclosure is almost exactly the size of the outer square at Kufa, but the material—small flat stones set in abundant mortar—recalls that of Qasr al-Kharanah. Also like Kharanah the east, west, and south portals are formed from split semicircular towers (plate 23).

Flanking the Court of Honor and the throne complex are four *bayts*. Each consists of two similar apartments facing north and south and probably used seasonally. The T-shaped spaces, flanked by rectangular rooms and separated from the courts by triple arcades, descend from a very ancient Mesopotamian and Persian house type. The north façade of the Court of Honor uses several types of blind arcading (plates 25, 27) which, like the lobed arches, were to have continued importance in later architecture. The fluted dome appears for the first time in Islam in the first cross passage beyond the entrance (plate 26). The great hall with its vast elliptical barrel vault suggests that the brick source of its design was undoubtedly Sassanian (plate 24). An innovation, later to be of great consequence, is the semicircular vault over a rectangular niche by which the north door is framed.

The Umayyad al-Walid, in addition to the mosque at Damascus, also built a congregational mosque, al-Aqsa, on the Haram as Sharif in Jerusalem. This building, severely damaged by the earthquake of 747–48, was entirely rebuilt by the Abbasid Caliph al-Mahdi (775–85) in 780. Al-Mahdi's mosque was in turn rebuilt in 1035 by the Fatimid Caliph as-Zahir, but he seems to have respected the main lines of the work of al-Mahdi, only reducing the number of aisles. This mosque occupies part of the south wall of the Haram as Sharif and is almost exactly oriented upon the Dome of the Rock (plate 2). The rest of the vast area, partly surrounded by arcades, corresponds to an immense *sahn*. Al-Mahdi's mosque had parallel aisles running north-south. The center was much wider than the previous version and was provided with a clerestory. Over the *mihrab* was a wooden dome (plate 28). Al-Aqsa, in its alignment on the Dome of the Rock, seems to have intentionally imitated the basilica aligned upon the Holy Sepulcher. Very probably the north-south aisles of the mosque at Cordoba of 785 were inspired by al-Aqsa (plate 29).

The Great Mosque at Qairawan, Tunisia, is considered the ancestor of all the other North African congregational mosques. It probably reached its present size under the Umayyad Caliph Hisham (724–43) to whose reign at least the lower portion of the minaret (plate 33) may belong. Since then there have been at least two complete reconstructions, the last by the Aghlabid Emir, Ziyadet Allah, in 836. The aisles, as in the al-Aqsa, run perpendicular to the *qibla* wall, from which they are separated by a cross corridor (plate 32). The masonry dome over the *mihrab*, which probably replaced an earlier wooden version, was added in 862 (plates 30, 31).

In 813, when the Caliph al-Amin was defeated and killed by his brother, al-Ma'mun, who had been living at Merv in Persia, a new wave of Persian influence was brought to Baghdad. Succeeding al-Ma'mun, al-Mu'tasim (833–42) surrounded himself with a praetorian guard of young Turkish slaves, whose descendants, in the next century, were to make and unmake caliphs at will. Soon there was so much strife between al-Mu'tasim's Turks and the people of Baghdad that he founded, in 836, a new capital at Samarra, a few miles north. There, with room to plan on a large scale, the slaves' quarters and the residences of the townspeople could be widely separated.

The result was an improvisation of unbaked brick, stucco, and wood, built in haste and of an almost incredible size. The central core of the Caliph's palace, the Jausaq al-Kharqani, is about 655 feet square (plate 35). A great flight of marble steps led to the triple-arched Bab al-Amma, the gate of public audience (plate 34). Retired behind the courts was the throne room, a domed square surrounded by four basilical halls, each preceded by a transverse chamber recalling the T-shaped rooms at Ukhaidir. The complex plan reflects the involved court ceremonial which was rapidly surrounding the caliph with godlike honors.

The Bulkawara Palace at Samarra, built for a son of the Caliph al-Mutawakkil (847–61) between 849 and 859, has an outer enclosure 4100 feet square and an inner enclosure of ca. 1500 by 1900 feet which fronts the Tigris (plate 36). From the north gate a succession of three courts of honor, all made cruciform with intersecting paths or water courses, leads to the cruciform throne complex through triple-arched *iwans*. Niches of very intricate shapes and carved, molded stucco played an important part in the ornament (plate 37), but glass mosaic of vine tendrils in many shades of green and mother-of-pearl on a gold ground covered the triple entrance facing the river. Beside the river a quadripartite garden flanked by pavilions overlooking the water was probably an intentional evocation of the Koran's paradise suggested also by the mosaic vines of the nearby portal.

Begun in 847 by the Caliph al-Mutawakkil, the Great Mosque of Samarra, a burnt brick structure, recalls ancient Iraq in its material and in its extraordinary helicoid minaret (plate 38) after the model of a ziggurat. The mosque proper, of 784 by 512 feet, was insulated from the city around it by an outer court, or *ziyadah*, more than a fifth of a mile square. The flat wooden roof was supported directly, without arcades, by compound piers of stuccoed brick with slender marble shafts at the four corners, like the stone piers at Khirbet al-Mafjar. The interior must have been a bewildering, almost directionless maze, made more confusing by the remarkable number of portals.

Ahmad Ibn Tulun, appointed governor of Egypt in 869 at the age of 34, was the son of a Turkish slave of the Caliph al-

Ma'mun. His mosque, finished in 879, introduced Cairo to several new ideas from Samarra. The plan of Ibn Tulun–with its many portals and *ziyadah* (plate 40)–the spiral minaret, and the use of compound piers in stuccoed brick were all imports from Samarra (plate 41). The mosque has been badly damaged and often restored, but enough of the stucco ornament remains to show the combination of motifs from Samarra, primarily Sassanian, and local survivals, primarily of Hellenistic origin. A view of the roofless arcades before the last restoration shows the remains of the great inscription on wood which encircled the building several times just under the roof (plate 43). The solemn progression of gently pointed arches controls movement and vision. Since the piers are thick enough to discourage an oblique view, each aisle is like a broad corridor. The visitor must come to a halt and reorient himself where the ranges intersect (plate 42).

In examining all of these architectural monuments, one can already see the fusion of elements from several styles. The first Muslim armies, beginning their campaigns from Medina, encroached upon the preserves of two major ancient civilizations. Those who went north to spread into North Africa, Egypt, Palestine, and Syria entered a strongly Hellenized area whose ties with Greek and Roman civilization had been strengthened by Christianity. The first Arab monuments there, the Dome of the Rock and the Great Mosque of Damascus, borrowed liberally from these sources. As long as the Umayyad regime survived, Syrian Hellenism played an important role but the mixture of styles at Khirbet al-Mafjar shows that it did not go unchallenged. In the south the conquest of the Sassanian Kingdom brought Islam into contact with a civilization based both on orientalized Hellenism and on the resurgence of ancient Iraqi culture. Certainly what cultural traditions the Arabs brought were more akin to this world than to the more Hellenized northern regions. Furthermore, the Sassanians seem to have preserved many nomad traditions of their own. The great reliefs at Tak i-Bostan and elsewhere glorify the royal hunts conducted in enclosed game preserves and this custom must have pleased the new rulers, since facilities for similar hunts seem to have been provided at many of their country palaces. One has only to look at the crude fixed stare of the great-eyed stucco sculptures at Khirbet al-Mafjar to realize how closely related they are to ancient Sumerian votive statues.

19

Sa'd ibn al Waqqas' emulation of the pomp of his Sassanian predecessors misfired, and the Umayyads seem never again to have attempted anything so elaborate until the unfinished palace at Mshatta, at the very end of their regime. Nevertheless, the form survived and flowered in the fantastic Abbasid palaces at Samarra. Because of the discovery of Kufa, these need no longer be considered new Persian imports; the pattern had actually never left Iraq. The strict symmetry of most Arab palaces from Kufa to Samarra is ultimately of Roman origin, but was probably inherited from the Sassanians. It was apparently stronger in Iraq, if we compare Kufa to Khirbet al-Mafjar, than in the more Hellenized area of Palestine.

The use of ornament as an aid to religious contemplation cannot easily be traced in this period. Neither at the Dome of the Rock nor in the Great Mosque at Damascus does it appear to have fully achieved this function. In both these monuments the mosaics have not yet lost the illusionistic elements of Hellenistic and Roman times. The abstract patterns of the quartered marble below them, where it survives, would seem to have been more inspiring to later decorators than were the mosaics themselves. At Khirbet al-Mafjar, however, abstract interlaced patterns compete with naturalistic vine scrolls, and in doing so undergo a transformation away from their illusionistic origins. Nothing remains of the once elaborate ornament of the Great Mosque of Samarra; but Ibn Tulun's mosque, damaged as it is, has already achieved the Islamic ideal of a refuge formed of endlessly repeated, hypnotically identical, shapes and spaces. The abstract continuous patterns of the Bulkawara Palace stuccoes are there exploited in an endless demonstration of the oneness of God.

The development of both mosque and palace, therefore, seems to owe much more to Iraq and Persian sources than to Syrian Hellenism. Indeed the pointed arch itself, intentionally produced in cut stone at Khirbet al-Mafjar, is probably derived from parabolic arches of brick used by the Sassanians, as is the vault of the great hall at Ukhaidir. Just as the Sassanians had orientalized Parthian civilization so, ultimately, the Arabs orientalized the former Byzantine provinces from North Africa to Syria. For nearly eight centuries, although Islamic and Western architecture exchanged a few minor details or techniques, they remained oil and water so far as significant mutual influence was concerned.[11]

2 THE ARCHITECTURE
OF NORTH AFRICA AND SPAIN

The only member of the Umayyad family to escape the Abbasid Massacre was Abd er-Rahman, grandson of the Caliph Hisham, who established himself as Emir of Cordoba in 756. In 926 his descendant, Abd er-Rahman III, assumed the title of Caliph, so that Islam was divided into three parts: Umayyad, Abbasid and Fatimid. The Umayyads, with their Syrian followers in Spain, continued the development of Umayyad architecture in North Africa and Spain until the abolition of the caliphate in 1031, by which date the empire had collapsed into quarreling petty states.

The Great Friday Mosque at Cordoba, although mutilated by sixteenth-century additions, is one of the finest surviving works of Islamic architecture. Throughout four successive enlargements it retained a remarkable unity of style (plate 44). The first mosque which had no arcades around the *sahn*, begun in 785 by Abd er-Rahman I, set the pattern of parallel north-south aisles followed by most North African mosques. The design of the extraordinary double-tiered arches, banded in brick and stone, which support the wooden ceiling (plate 45) was also established at this time, perhaps after the pattern of a Roman aqueduct. The problem these arches solve, that of adjusting the short antique column shafts to a high ceiling, had been met before at Damascus by the use of double tiers of arches (plate 9). Their rounded horseshoe shape had appeared occasionally in earlier Umayyad architecture, but only in Spain and North Africa did it become so widespread. In 848 Abd er-Rahman II extended the prayer hall eight bays to the south; Abd er-Rahman III enlarged the *sahn* and built the present minaret; and by 952 the *sahn* had been surrounded with arcades. But it was under Hakam II, between 961 and 968, that the most beautiful parts of the building were completed. These include the three vaults over the *maqsura* and the splendid lantern on axis with the *mihrab* at the beginning of Hakam's addition (plate 47). Finally, in 987, al-Mansur began the eight eastern aisles and widened the *sahn*, bringing the structure to its present dimensions of about 445 by 610 feet.

With Hakam II's work Umayyad architecture reached its apogee. He was probably inspired by the additions made a century before to the mosque at Qairawan, where stone vaults were added, as at Cordoba, to a columnar structure (plate 30). The dome over the *mihrab* bay at Qairawan is deeply gored, as is its somewhat later companion over the last bay of the same aisle next to the *sahn*. Miniature domes of the same pattern terminate the vaults of the lantern and the *mihrab* bay at Cordoba (plate 50). In Roman times, the fluted dome had been symbolically associated with the vault of Heaven and in Byzantine churches and palaces it carried the same meaning. The fluted dome at Ukhaidir covered the major ceremonial passage of a palace, and probably retained its ancient connotation. At Qairawan, and later at Cordoba, fluted domes crown the center aisles of Friday mosques in the capitals of two autocrats, who still must sometimes have conducted the Friday prayer under them. Thus, it can be inferred that the symbolic association of the gored dome with sovereignty was still known to the architect of Cordoba and his patron.

The variety of angular interlace in the ornament of Khirbet al-Mafjar is less common at Cordoba, where plant forms dominate. Nevertheless, Hakam's architect used the principle of the interlace far more audaciously than had any of his predecessors. In order to secure his four vaults on a system unsuited to support them, he provided cross-bracing by interlacing the double tiers of arches themselves, at the same time producing decorative lobate profiles (plate 48). The vaults are composed of arches interlaced in three dimensions—a technique which may have originated in the brick architecture of Persia and which perhaps influenced the development of the much later Western rib vault (plate 49). At Cordoba the bewildering multiplicity of arched supports and the nervous, almost staccato, punctuation of space are both disturbing and hypnotic in contrast to the ponderous divisions of Ibn Tulun's mosque. The infinite complexity of structure assumes an active rather than a passive role. Here, the worshiper is enmeshed in the acts of God whose fervent, emotional aura can be felt in Andalusia today.

In contrast, the exterior is static (plate 46). Even the portals are flat against the wall, their ornament not so much built as inscribed. Buttresses uniformly articulate the wall, recalling the projecting towers of Umayyad palaces, and, like them, having no reference to the structure within.

Near Cordoba, in 936, Abd er-Rahman III founded a new city, Medina az-Zahra, to house not only his residence, but his government. This was not the hasty improvisation of Samarra, but solid building of cut-stone masonry and marble, fully in the Syrian tradition. Burned and sacked in 1010, the town was soon deserted. The ruins form a rectangle of about 5000 by 2450 feet, of which only a small section of the palace has been excavated (plate 51). These buildings begin at the north wall and descend southward in at least three terraces. As a whole, they have none of the axial symmetry of the Samarra palaces, but form a series of loosely connected units each with its square patio. At the eastern limits of the excavated area are two basilical halls, each facing a patio. Both are tripartite like Mshatta or Kufa, and both open onto their courts through a transverse space like the T-shaped rooms at Ukhaidir and Samarra. If domes were ever associated with these structures they were of wood and have been completely destroyed.

The hall to the lower right of the plan, discovered in 1944, was of exceptional richness. The decoration that at Samarra was in stucco is here replaced by marble and limestone. Enough fragments have been recovered to allow a restoration which shows that, as at Cordoba, columns supporting horseshoe arches with sculptured voussoirs were used (plate 53). At Medina az-Zahra, however, column bases appear as antique in character as the composite capitals. The panels of ornament forming dadoes around the walls and covering pilasters are nearly all of vegetable origin (plate 52). Usually each panel contains a single stalk whose leaves and fruit curl symmetrically. The carving is crisp, employing deep undercutting and creating a high contrast of light and dark. Geometric forms occupy subordinate positions and there is little interlace. Except for this change in emphasis, the ornament is clearly derived from that of Khirbet al-Mafjar. The two hundred or so years between seem to have produced surprisingly few changes.

23

THE ALMORAVIDS IN NORTH AFRICA (1031–ca. 1150)

A group of Berber tribes from the Sahara had, since the mid-eleventh century, subdued all North Africa. They were puritans and religious fanatics who, when asked for help by the petty states into which the Spanish Umayyad empire had collapsed, remained to rule. But even they soon succumbed to Andalusian luxury, as their major architectural monuments demonstrate.

Between 1135 and 1143, under the Almoravid Emir, Ali ben Yousof, the Qarawiyin Mosque in Fez was enlarged and the *mihrab* aisle provided with vaults in plaster, suspended from wooden frames and therefore totally nonstructural. One of these is a domical "stalactite" vault of a form so universal in later Islamic architecture that a brief discussion of its origin is necessary here (plate 54).

The stalactite vault should more accurately be called by the Arabic term, *muqarnas*, which comes probably from the same late Greek root as our "cornice," originally meaning "scale-shaped roof." Its origin is still obscure, but almost certainly it began in brick architecture as a by-product of the elaboration of the squinch used to transform a square into the circular base for a dome. The earliest such multiple squinch presently known appears at Yazd in Persia in the tomb of Duvazda-i Iman, of 1037. By the late eleventh century *muqarnas* units are employed in stone carved cornices and niche heads in Anatolia, Syria, and Egypt. At the same time in Iraq, near Samarra, the first known full *muqarnas* dome in brick and stucco was under construction.

Ali ben Yousof, in 1136, also ordered the decoration of the center aisle of the Mosque at Tlemcen, where the vault over the *mihrab* is braced by twelve interlaced arches instead of eight as at Fez and at Cordoba (plate 55). The *muqarnas* vaults in the four corners and the cupola could be expected after Fez, but the startling use of pierced stucco webbing between the ribs lighted from above is unique. It seems hard to believe that this structure is not a reconstruction of the thirteenth century when such reduction of forms, from the structural to the purely decorative, was more common.

24   THE ALMOHADS IN NORTH AFRICA AND SPAIN (ca. 1150–ca.1250)

At the beginning of the twelfth century the Almohads, a fundamentalist Muslim sect among the Berbers of the Atlas Mountains, began to expand at the expense of the Almoravids. By mid-century they ruled North Africa and a few years later were called to Spain to fight the Christians as the Almoravids had been before them. Following their predecessors' pattern, they remained to rule.

The Almohads made Tinmal their first capital and there in 1153, they built a now-ruined congregational mosque of brick and plaster whose horseshoe arches were consistently pointed rather than round as at Cordoba and Tlemcen. In contrast with Tlemcen's, the *mihrab* is ornamented with sober, large-scale moldings, carefully proportioned (compare plates 56 and 58). The "lambrequin arch" (plate 57), which was to become important, appears here for the first time. It probably developed from the lobed arch in combination with the *muqarnas*. The soberness found in Tinmal is also apparent in the Kutubiyya Mosque at Marrakesh of about the same date (plate 59). The rhythmic succession of pointed arches stripped of all ornament is in sharp contrast to the nervous profusion of Cordoba.

Of the Congregational Mosque of Seville, built by the Almohads between 1172 and 1176, only part of the *sahn* survives, the rest of the mosque having been replaced by a fifteenth-century cathedral (plate 60). The massive arcade of pointed horseshoe arches in bare brick, although heavily restored, retains the essential character of the original structure. The famous minaret, begun at the same time as the mosque and, like it, built entirely of brick, was finished in 1195 (plate 61).[12] As in all North African minarets, the Syrian Christian tradition of the square tower with arcaded windows was followed. The panels of interlaced arches, developed from those at Cordoba, follow the pattern of the stucco panels flanking the *mihrab* at Tinmal. The transformation of an originally structural form into a purely decorative one occurs here as it did in the *mihrab* vault at Tlemcen. At Seville, however, the scale is large and the relief high. Visually, the effect is vigorous and superbly suited to the brilliant sunlight in which the Giralda tower is usually seen.

THE MERINIDS IN NORTH AFRICA (ca. 1250–ca. 1350)

The Almohad empire collapsed early in the thirteenth century, leaving in its wake nearly eighty years of chaos. As a result, little building went on until the Merinids of Fez established themselves as the strongest of several small dynasties. The Merinids were warlike and religious, concerning themselves with pious foundations rather than with palaces.

The Mosque at Taza, with its *mihrab* vault of carved stucco, was begun by order of the Merinid Emir Abou Ya'qoub in 1291 and finished the following year (plate 62). The design is based upon the interlaced arches of one of the vaults at Cordoba (plate 49). However, the transformation of the once-structural idea to a decorative one has progressed much further than the stage reached at Tlemcen (plate 55). Carved plaster provides a superb medium for lavish ornament, but the planar discipline characteristic of Islamic architectural design has here reduced everything except the *muqarnas* squinches to a kind of fretted texture. At the same time the scale of the individual parts has been much reduced, thus accelerating a process which had been going on for some time. For example, in the original model at Cordoba, eight interlacing arches produced eight panels. At Tlemcen there were twelve arches and twelve panels. At Taza, however, there are sixteen panels and the "arches" which form them no longer even connect in the center. Thus, the structural form has been reduced to a marvelously complex interlace.

The madrasa, a religious school for the teaching of Sunni doctrine, was introduced into North Africa in the thirteenth century. It originated in Persia and was developed in Syria, Egypt, and Turkey; but it was the Syrian type which appeared in North Africa. The Bou Inaniya Madrasa at Fez, built for Abou Inan between 1350 and 1355, is the most monumental of all these North African foundations. Its plan consists of a *sahn* surrounded by galleries closed off by wooden screens and oriented toward a prayer hall opposite the monumental entrance (plate 63). The court is flanked by two square lecture halls lighted from above and separated from the court by huge wooden doors (plate 64). The cruciform plan includes on one axis the portal and the spacious prayer hall with its transverse arcade, both of Syrian origin (see plate 101). In the prayer hall, the very slightly pointed arches retain their horseshoe shape, and the treatment of the *mihrab* is distinctly Cordoban. In the court, however, the horseshoe arch disappears in favor of lambrequin arches and lobate forms, only slightly pointed. The court is treated as a continuous arcade with a second story inserted, resting on wooden lintels supported by corbels. This motif suggests the Egyptian practice, current since the thirteenth century, of articulating an exterior wall into two-story bays by means of sunken panels surmounted by *muqarnas* ornament.

THE NAZARI KINGDOM OF GRANADA AND THE ALHAMBRA (1238–1492)

The most powerful of the Spanish kingdoms after the collapse of the Almohad Empire was that founded by Muhammad Ibn al-Ahmar (1232–73) at Granada in 1238, two years after the fall of Cordoba to the Christians and a decade before that of Seville. Briefly, before the final conquest of Granada in 1492, the intellectual and artistic glories of the Umayyad court at Cordoba were revived at Granada. There the Alhambra, the oldest well-preserved Islamic palace in the world, remains to testify to the extraordinary elegance of the last Moorish civilization in Europe.

This palace, adjacent as at Medina az-Zahra to the north wall of the citadel, consists of two major units, each surrounding a rectangular court (plate 65). The first of these consists of the Court of Myrtles, or Alberca—named from the large pool which almost fills it—and its surrounding apartments, including the Hall of the Ambassadors in the Tower of Comares. Although some of the decoration may have been later, the construction was almost certainly during the reign of Yusuf the First. The Hall of the Ambassadors, the north terminus of the axis around which the plan is symmetrically disposed, was once the throne room (plate 66). Its present pavilion-like appearance, commanding magnificent views of the valley, must be very unlike what it once was. All the stucco ornament, carved with incredible intricacy on a scale so minute it looks like embroidered cloth, was once brilliantly colored and gilded, and the windows were filled with stained glass set in plaster. The wooden *muqarnas* cornice under the ceiling was once gilded as was the wood-paneled cloister vault above it. The rich gloom of this chamber in its original state must have provided a striking contrast to the brilliantly sunlit court beyond with its sparkling pool. There was little provision for large numbers of courtiers, since this was a small embattled kingdom at the edge of a hostile continent.

The contrasting axis of the Court of Lions and its lack of direct communication with the Court of Myrtles have led to the suggestion that one was used in summer and the other in winter, or that one was for public, and the other for private, use. The second suggestion, as will appear, seems more likely. The fact that the Hall of the Two Sisters comprises a square inner chamber with four doors and a dome, suggesting a throne complex like Kufa or Ukhaidir, would not be incompatible with such private use. In any event, the apartments are so small as to preclude a large public assemblage.

The cruciform plan with four water channels and a central fountain goes back at least to Samarra. Since a similar court, much ruined, at Murcia dates from the twelfth century, the scheme was probably introduced from North Africa by the Almoravids. The long room at the west end of the court, the Hall of Justice, is lighted by three square lanterns roofed with *muqarnas* vaults in plaster. They divide the chamber into compartments by means of lambrequin arches entirely of *muqarnas* (plate 69). The arcades of the Court of Lions are extremely complex (plate 67). Their columns–single, paired, triple and, where the east and west pavilions project, quadruple –create an extraordinary effect of massed verticals. This is counteracted by the projecting eaves, essential to the protection of the stucco arches. The incised ornament of the spandrels is pierced through, thus showing all the arcades to have become mere ornamental embellishments to an essentially trabeated wooden frame structure. The two pavilions employ only lambrequin arches of *muqarnas*, and both ends of the north and south arcades are treated identically. If one stands behind these and looks across, there appears a bewildering succession of lacelike filigrees in which the architecture seems as insubstantial as a cloud.

At the south terminal of the north-south axis is the Hall of the Abencerages, whose vault is perhaps the most fantastic in Islam, if not in the world (plate 68). *Muqarnas* "squinches" project from the walls, giving a square the shape of an eight-pointed star. The star is then extended into a "drum" with sixteen windows and closed by a *muqarnas* dome of infinite complexity. Here Islamic imagination reaches an apex of illusion. Structure has no meaning at all, the entire vault being suspended from a concealed wooden frame. What shows, however, is so eaten away by its own design as to become immaterial as mist. If, as appears to be the case, the aim of Islamic ornament is to dematerialize the surfaces it covers, the Court of Lions is literally the ultimate possible development in terms of carved stucco. The interiors seem not so much to rest upon the earth as to hover over it.

The complex of the Court of Lions seems to be the best expression of an ideal tenaciously held in the mind of the Islamic patron and his architect: space is always interior and its boundaries are to be clearly defined. Vistas of successive spaces are tolerated only if they are repetitious. A series of identical spaces as in the Hall of Justice is divided by identical screens. Non-identical spaces are so arranged that one cannot be seen from the other. There is no interest whatever in expressing structure either actually or symbolically. Visual effect is of paramount importance; and to this end lighting, generally from above, is carefully controlled. It should be remembered that these complex spaces were usually to be enjoyed by persons seated on or near the marble floors. From this position the ornament appears at its best, and the fantastic ceilings are most prominent. The same factor governed the design of the innumerable fountains, all set close to the pavement where the spray from their jets would be most refreshing.

The Koran's descriptions of paradise have already been mentioned. The Court of Lions corresponds very closely to them. It is shut off from the outer world; it has four "rivers" running down to the central fountain and innumerable "springs." Above all, however, is the actual attempt to make walls and ceilings immaterial, as though they too corresponded to an idea: the shadow of a greater reality awaiting the believer in the after-life. Since paradise is eternal, it may be that the curious method of space compartmentation here has symbolic value. A modulated series of successively changing spaces, frequent in Western architecture, implies the passage of time; but a series of identical spaces does not, nor does the abrupt transition from one to another. We may infer that Muhammad V, for his private apartments, chose to dwell in a timeless paradise; a paradise timeless, too, for his successors during another century, until ended forever by Ferdinand of Aragon and Isabella of Castile.

North African and Spanish Islamic architecture, more than that of Egypt, Syria, or Turkey, tended to develop isolated from the rest of Islam. The Umayyads of Cordoba continued the style and the structural methods of their Syrian ancestors. Except for a change in the shape of the arch the columned halls of Syria, roofed in wood, continued to the end. The Medina az-Zahra Palace might be so many square Syrian mansions, grouped loosely together. What was new was the heightened emotion of the complex interplay of structure in the Great Mosque at Cordoba.

After the fall of the Umayyad dynasty, new ideas were imported into North Africa, ultimately from Iraq. Among them were brick-piered congregational mosques, the pointed arch (retaining, however, its horseshoe shape), *muqarnas* work, and the extensive use of carved plaster. These had blended with the older style by the thirteenth century and then flowered in the fourteenth in the Alhambra, again in isolation from the rest of the Muslim world. The final result was an architecture, on a relatively small scale, of total fantasy, utterly remote from practicality—the too-polished jewel of a civilization which knew its days were numbered.

3

THE ARCHITECTURE
OF EGYPT

THE FATIMID DYNASTY (969–1171)

The Fatimids, who conquered Egypt in 969 and established their capital on the site of modern Cairo, belonged to the Shi'ite sect and claimed to trace their descent through the last Orthodox Caliph, Ali. Though this sect was always strongest in Persia, the Fatimids came to power in the early tenth century in North Africa. The only surviving major monument of their North African years is the north portal of the Mosque of Mahdiya (plate 70), the capital they founded in 912-13. This structure marks the earliest use of a projecting monumental portal since that of the bath at Khirbet al-Mafjar. It has been compared to Roman triumphal arches, of whose imperial associations Ubayd Allah, founder of the dynasty and leader of the Friday prayer in the mosque, may have been aware. Of the great palace the Fatimids built at Cairo, nothing remains save a few carved beams, but a writer of the thirteenth century who saw it said there were twelve square pavilions touching each other and built of stone.[13] This sounds a little like a description of the almost contemporary Palace of Medina az-Zahra and would be in keeping with the North African origins of the dynasty.

The earliest surviving Fatimid structure in Cairo is the Congregational Mosque of al-Azhar, founded in 970, which in 988 began its career as the great Muslim University of today. In this process the building's original appearance was almost entirely lost. Creswell's proposed reconstruction of the plan leaves undecided all questions as to the exterior walls (plate 71). The use of columns, clerestoried *mihrab* nave, and aisles parallel to the *qibla* wall all suggest an Umayyad though not a specifically North African Umayyad influence or revival (plate 73). Another arcade, not shown in the plan, was added all around the *sahn* between 1130 and 1149 (plate 72). By this time the keel-shaped arch, introduced perhaps from Iraq, had replaced nearly all other forms in Cairo.

Begun in 990, the Mosque of al-Hakim was in use a year later, but the monumental entrance and the two minarets of the north façade were begun under the Caliph al-Hakim in 1003 and finished only in ten years. The structure was modeled on that of Ibn Tulun, with arcades supported on brick compound piers, but the three domes of the *qibla* aisle and the clerestoried *mihrab* nave follow al-Azhar. The superb masonry of the monumental entrance and the two minarets, recalling Mahdiya, are unprecedented in Egypt. The crisp vigorous sculpture suggests the work at Medina az-Zahra of about fifty years before (plates 74-75).

The suburb of al-Fustat, founded in the seventh century by Amr ibn al-As, flourished until the famine, pestilence, and riots of the mid-eleventh century caused its abandonment. The excavated remains probably belong to the latter part of this period. Little more than traces of walls generally survive but enough for plans to be drawn from them. At least one house had a court with an elaborate water system and rooms on either end (plate 76), very like the summer and winter quarters of the *bayts* at Ukhaidir. A smaller establishment has a four-*iwan* court (plate 77) which, though on a minute scale, suggests the court of honor at Kufa.

Weakened by the economic troubles of the mid-century, the Fatimid Caliphs, like their Sunni rivals in Baghdad, began to be menaced by their Turkish slave guards. To offset this menace, the Fatimid al-Mustansir in 1073 called in the Armenian General Badr al-Gamali. In 1087 Badr strengthened and extended the walls of Cairo, replacing the mud brick with some of the finest masonry ever erected. The Bab al-Futuh (plates 78, 79) is one of the gates designed for Badr by three Christian brothers, all architects, from Urfa (Edessa). The design of the gate is closely related to North Syria and Armenia where semicircular arches and spherical pendentives in stone were common. The cushion voussoirs of the niches flanking the portal and the curious panels of knotted molding above, which appear here for the first time in Egypt, may represent an Umayyad survival in Syria, insofar as similar forms appear at Khirbet al-Mafjar.

The last important monument of the later Fatimid period is the Mosque of al-Aqmar completed in 1125. The originally symmetrical façade exhibits the first use in Egypt of the keel-shaped arch in combination with a ribbed niche head (plate 81). The same arch appeared in brick on the Baghdad Gate of Raqqa of 772 (plate 39) where it also framed lobed niches with ribbing behind. To the Fatimids, or perhaps to their Syrian or Armenian stone masons, must be given the credit of translating it into

31

excellent stone masonry. *Muqarnas* ornament lines the niche heads flanking the portal, as it had done when it first appeared in Egypt in the 1080's in a niche of the Bab al-Futuh.[14]

THE AYYUBID DYNASTY (1171–1250)

The famous Salah ad-Din (1138–93) ended the line of Fatimid Caliphs in 1171 when he restored the Abbasid Caliph's name to the Friday Prayer. Himself a Kurd from North Syria, Saladin, as he was all too well known by the Crusaders, had been reared among Seljuk Turks, all ardent Sunni Muslims and supporters of the Abbasids. It was he who introduced the madrasa into Egypt. Unfortunately, nothing remains of Salah ad-Din's madrasas, and the citadel he began has been much altered. However, the madrasa founded by Sultan Salih Negm ad-Din (1242–43/44) suggests what the earlier ones may have been like.

The façade of this great building marks a new emphasis on public appearance and the planning of an urban environment (plate 80). The whole was once visible as a decorated wall bordering a relatively wide space, later further defined by monumental façades on its west side. The center portal, repeating on a larger scale that of the Mosque of al-Aqmar, stands over a public street, to the north and south of which lie the two sections of the madrasa. Each section consists of a rectangular *sahn* defined to north and south by students' cells and to east and west by barrel-vaulted *iwans*. In order that the *iwan*-prayer halls should face Mecca they are out of alignment with the street.

The earliest madrasas in Khorassan were often established in the former dwellings of their patrons. This is known to have happened also in Cairo, and although Sultan Salih's madrasa was never a dwelling, the plan of its teaching units suggests the qa'a, or reception hall, of a type of Egyptian house which had been current from at least the first half of the twelfth century (plate 94).[15] As in all later Egyptian madrasas, as well as private houses, access was never direct but always through a baffled corridor. Neither was it ever directly into an *iwan* but always into the *sahn*. At least in Egypt there was good reason for this, because each *iwan* was usually reserved for the use of one of the four schools of Sunni doctrine: Shafeyite, Malikite, Hanafite or Hanbalite. Sultan Salih was the first to establish courses for all four schools in one place. His tomb, to the left of his madrasa, was completed in 1250. Square domed tomb-chambers, either free-standing or attached to the pious foundations of the deceased, were the standard type of Islamic funeral monument in Egypt at all periods.

THE MAMLUK DYNASTIES (1250–1517)

The word *mamluk*, derived from the verb "to own" was used for white male slaves either captured in war or purchased. There were two Mamluk dynasties. The Bahris (1250–1390), mostly Turks and Mongols, who belonged to Sultan Salih, became his generals and inherited his throne soon after his death. The Burji Mamluks (1382–1717), mostly Circassian, had been bought by the Bahri Mamluk Sultan, Qala'un. Succession in both dynasties was more often by murder and usurpation than by inheritance, and the average reign of any sultan was only six years. Despite these chaotic political conditions, architecture flourished and evolved new forms, though without any significant break between the two dynasties, even after the Turkish conquest of 1517 had brought an end to Egyptian independence.

The first great Mamluk sultan was Baybars al-Bunduqdari (1260–77). He practically completed the expulsion of the last Crusaders, saved Egypt from the Mongols, and re-established the Abbasid caliphs in Cairo after the fall of Baghdad. Only the outer walls of his congregational mosque (1267–69) remain, but the plan can be traced (plate 83). Like Hakim's mosque in its projecting portals and corner towers, Baybars' had only one minaret over the north portal, and columns as well as brick piers supported its arcades (plate 82). The arches are stilted and pointed throughout, the keel-shaped arch being used only for decorative niches, a role it was never to lose. The great *maqsura*, once covered with a wooden dome and approached by a basilical nave with a clerestory, is unique in Egypt and probably of North Syrian origin. Cairo was then receiving a substantial increase in population from the Syrian, Iraqi, and even Anatolian refugees who were fleeing from the Mongols before and after the destruction of Baghdad in 1258.

Built in little more than a year between 1284 and 1285, the Madrasa and Tomb of the Sultan Qala'un complex included a *maristan*, or hospital, now almost wholly destroyed and omitted in the plan (plate 85). Like Sultan Salih's madrasa, which it faces, it has a monumental public façade which hides an interior whose orientation toward Mecca demanded considerable adjustment (plate 84). The double round arched windows with oculi above framed by deeply recessed pointed archivolts suggest late

Romanesque architecture of the West[16] and give the façade a plasticity usually lacking in Islam. The basilical south *iwan* suggests a possible derivation from palace architecture. The latter may well have continued to influence the design even of madrasas built as such. The tomb is square and supports a dome (a modern restoration) on a combination of piers and columns. The scheme as a whole was probably inspired by that of the Dome of the Rock, well known to the Sultan. The extreme richness of the stone intarsia, plaster, and wood ornament gives an unforgettable impression of splendor only half revealed by light filtered by thick grills of plaster set with colored glass. The cenotaph is surrounded by a high *maqsura* of *mushrabiyya*, a kind of turned wooden screenwork. This so obstructs circulation that nowhere can one gain a complete view of the space (plate 86). As a result, the relatively small interior seems endless.

The most impressive monument in Cairo, the Madrasa of Sultan Hasan begun in 1356, was finished in 1362/63 after the Sultan's death. It is a cruciform madrasa enlarged to enormous scale, the *sahn* measuring about 100 feet square (plate 87). The first madrasa in Egypt with four *iwans* was that of Baybars of 1262–63, now almost completely destroyed, and the second that of Sultan an-Nasir begun in 1296. Like all its Egyptian predecessors, that of Hasan carefully avoids direct entrance into any *iwan*. In this it is quite unlike most Syrian or Seljuk Turkish madrasas; but Persian precedent probably dictated the placing of the domed tomb-chamber directly behind the *qibla iwan*.

The *muqarnas* portal is truly colossal, rising 66 feet above the pavement and set in a cliff of masonry 113 feet to the top of its enormous cornice (plate 89).[17] The *sahn* is one of the most magnificent spaces in all Islamic architecture (plate 88). It is an almost perfect cube, so deep as seldom to admit direct sunlight to its center. The four *iwans* puncture the vast wall surfaces, unrelieved by any transition save their polychrome voussoirs. Only the exuberant curves of the fountain pavilion relieve the general solemnity, aided by the fleur-de-lys crenelations which almost universally replaced the stepped Sassanian forms which had been favored by Umayyads and Abbasids alike.

From the point of view of elegance and refinement, the reign of Sultan Qayt Bay (1468–96) marked the greatest epoch of Egyptian architecture, of which his tomb-madrasa is the finest single building. Composite in function, it includes a four-*iwan* madrasa, cells for students, a tomb, and a *sabil*, or public drinking fountain, with a boys' primary school in an open loggia above it (plate 91). The mastery of architectural composition, in the asymmetrical association of shapes expressing all these functions, is unequaled (plate 90). The same sureness of touch appears in the exact proportions of square, octagon, and cylinder of the exquisite minaret. The *sahn* has two wide *iwans* supported by pointed horseshoe arches[18] and two narrow ones with very stilted arches (plate 92). Everywhere reigns an elaborate polychromy of inlaid and encrusted stone and marble. The building, like the churches of Siena and Orvieto, is striped almost literally like a tiger, a technique which can ultimately be traced to the alternation of brick and stone in late Roman and Byzantine masonry. The use of marble marquetry was uncommon in Egypt until late Ayyubid times and probably received an impetus from Syrian refugees. As in any other technique, such virtuosity could be a pitfall, and Qayt Bay's madrasa approaches meaningless excess. The effect of the *sahn* was probably better when its wooden roof, which would have subdued the light, was intact.

The deliberately picturesque asymmetry of Qayt Bay's madrasa probably arose from the necessity of adapting many such structures to very restricted urban sites. Cairo, like other Muslim cities, originally had a few large *maydans*, or clear spaces, usually narrow rectangles within the walls. It was across one of these that Qala'un's Madrasa faced Sultan Salih's. During the city's decline these were built over with ramshackle structures. From the *maydans* radiated irregular alleys, nearly always blind and constantly made narrower and more tortuous by the unplanned accretion of private building. Within such a complex, the Madrasa and Tomb of Qani Bay Akhur was intended to be seen as it rose up out of dusty shadow to catch the sunlight in the elaborately carved stone ornament of its dome (plate 95). The street is shaded by the projecting upper floors of most of its houses, with their wooden or stone corbels and the even greater projections of *mushrabiyya* windows.

Domestic architecture changed remarkably little between the twelfth and the early nineteenth centuries, when the contemporary Turkish style was belatedly introduced. Gamal ad-Din az-Zahabi's town house could easily have been built three hundred years before its actual date of 1637. The exterior is very like those leading toward Qani Bay Akhur's tomb (plate 95), with only one opening at street level giving access through a baffled corridor to the *hosh* (plate 93). In the north wall of this inner court is the *maqad*, or open loggia, communicating with the major public rooms of the first floor. These were usually reached from the court by an outside stair leading to an elaborate portal, usually just to the right of the *maqad*. Here was the actual ceremonial entrance where the host might receive his male guests and conduct them to the *qa'a* (plate 94). This chamber usually consisted of a square, depressed central space, the *durqa*, extending up into a clerestory where the wooden roof might be domed. The guest stepped directly into the *durqa*, which might have a central fountain but whose marble floor was otherwise bare. He then found raised *iwans* to right and left, framed by carved and painted wooden arches. Removing his shoes, he stepped up to the *iwans*, whose floors were matted or carpeted, with padded benches around the walls. In more elaborate houses and palaces the *qa'a* was cruciform with four *iwans* around the *durqa*.

It is obvious that the *durqa* was once an open court like that of the houses at Fustat, also equipped with two to four *iwans*. These in turn relate to the houses of Samarra and to Ukhaidir, and through them to Sassanian and Parthian houses. No historical connection can yet be made between the Parthian cruciform court and the Roman atrium, but it seems clear they had the same ceremonial function, one which was preserved in Islamic domestic architecture well into the nineteenth century.

Egypt, Palestine, and Syria were, from the eleventh through the fifteenth century, far more closely linked than North Africa and Spain with the other portions of the Muslim world. The Fatimids first turned to local traditions in mosques such as al-Azhar and al-Hakim, though their workers must have had backgrounds which spread from Spain to North Syria. Beginning with Hakim's mosque, however, and vastly strengthened with the Bab al-Futuh of Badr al-Gamali, Syrian and Armenian masons began translating into stone forms originally built in brick. With the Ayyubids, the trend continued, given considerable impetus by refugees from Syria. Ornament became eclectic, borrowed from all parts of the Muslim world, including even Spain and North Africa, from which the horseshoe arch was imported in the late thirteenth century. In later Mamluk times the same reduction in scale of ornament in relation to architecture took place in Egypt as in Spain, and a certain preciousness appeared.

At all periods, however, Egyptian architecture maintained a strongly national character. Compared to that of North Africa it was virile and expansive, its ornament harsh and clear. The *muqarnas* portal and the use of stone masonry relate it to Seljuk architecture of the thirteenth century, but Egyptian architecture compares to that of the Seljuks much as the rather lean, spare design of fifteenth-century Spanish Gothic compares to the richer, more plastic Gothic architecture of Portugal.

4 ISLAMIC ARCHITECTURE UNDER TURKISH PATRONAGE

This study has already mentioned individuals of Turkish origin who played important roles as patrons of architecture; but their Turkish background was only incidental to their role as patrons. We have now to consider the architecture produced by and for descendants of non-Arab Turkish nomads who, by the tenth century, had embraced Islam and become ardent supporters of Sunni orthodoxy. Like the Arabs before Muhammad, the Turks had been wandering herdsmen, loosely associated in a complicated system of blood relationship. Their primitive shamanism, brought from Central Asia, had already been shaken by contacts with Buddhist, Christian, and Jewish, no less than with Muslim, missionaries.

Since the architecture of Persia is the subject of another volume of this series, the story of the Great Seljuks concerns us only as it affects Syria and the Seljuks of Rum, or Anatolia. The common ancestor of all the Seljuks, a member of the Guzz or Oguz tribe, from which the Ottoman Turks also descend, was a chieftain called Seljuk. He had four sons, Mikail, Yunus, Musa, and Israil, whose names suggest that Seljuk himself was not then a devout Muslim. Mikail's son, Tugrul (1031–63), captured Baghdad in 1055 and, although he needed an interpreter to communicate with the Caliph, he established his line as the protectors of the Abbasids. After the battle of Manzikert, Tugrul's nephew, Alp Arslan (1063–72), appointed Suleyman (1077–86), a grandson of Israil's, governor of Anatolia. Suleyman soon declared his independence and founded a dynasty which survived until 1308.

Alp Arslan's successor, Malik Shah, had a Turkish slave whose son, Zengi, became Governor of Mossul, where upon the dissolution of the Great Seljuks, he too founded a dynasty.

THE ZENGIDS OF MOSSUL (1127–1262)

Zengi's son, Nur ad-Din, took Damascus in 1154. The buildings he built there introduced forms employed for the Great Seljuks of Persia but often translated them into the masonry technique common to both Syria and Anatolia. One of Nur ad-Din's first acts after he had conquered Damascus was to endow a hospital (in Persian *maristan* and in Arabic *dar-as-shifa*). The work seems to have been finished rapidly and, except for paint and whitewash concealing the masonry, remains substantially as Nur ad-Din intended it to be. The plan (plate 98) shows a symmetrical arrangement of four *iwans* around a central court with a water tank. According to its inscription, the east *iwan* was certainly a consulting room, while the four vaulted corner chambers may have been wards. The portal stands within a shallow niche covered by a tiny fluted semidome whose *muqarnas* squinches have proliferated into a great frozen cascade (plate 97). They spring from a blind arcade of lobate arches like those at Samarra and Raqqa, whose proximity is probably responsible for the general concept.[19] The portal leads to a square antechamber with a full *muqarnas* vault, very tall and narrow, executed in plaster suspended from wooden beams. The method of lighting through openings pierced in the upper tiers of ornament, as well as by windows, suggests the *mihrab* dome at Tlemcen (compare plates 96 and 55). The west *iwan* is entered directly from the antechamber.

In 1172 Nur ad-Din endowed a madrasa and, on his death, was buried there under another fine *muqarnas* vault. The plan is cruciform in essence with an entrance directly into its eastern *iwan* (plate 99). This *iwan* leads to a rectangular *sahn* with a water basin fed by a wall fountain in the western *iwan*. Both east and west *iwans* have pointed stone barrel-vaults, but the north *iwan* has a wooden roof, as does the prayer-hall opposite which communicates with the *sahn* by three portals in the usual Syrian fashion.

Both of these buildings, the Madrasa and the Maristan, were adapted from the same basic cruciform plan. In Syria and in Anatolia there seems never to have been any thought of assigning each theological rite its own *iwan* in a madrasa as in Egypt.

38

Furthermore, one *iwan* was almost invariably used for the main entrance and another often for a fountain.

THE SELJUKS OF RUM (1071–1308)

Few of the many examples of twelfth-century Seljuk architecture in Anatolia have escaped extensive alteration.[20] The buildings of most importance to Islamic architectural history as a whole all belong to the culmination of Seljuk style in the last three quarters of the thirteenth century. Paradoxically, some of the best architecture was produced after 1242 when the Seljuk sultans had become vassals of the Mongols who ruled from Persia.

The Ulu Cami and Maristan at Divrigi, two structures in one, were begun in 1228/29 by Ahmet Shah, feudal lord of Divrigi under the Seljuk sultans (plate 101). The work is signed by the architect Khurrem Shah of Ahlat, son of Muhid of Ahlat. The mosque, of beautifully joined masonry, is roofed by complex stone rib vaults which were probably based on Persian originals of brick. They rested on columns, now concealed by later additions. The vault of the third bay of the center aisle had an oculus centered over a fountain like the impluvium of a Roman atrium. In all likelihood, this stood symbolically for the *sahn*, retained by congregational mosques built further south where the climate was milder. The extraordinary ornament of the north portal suggests the stuccoes of the mosque at Hamadan in Persia, but the carving close to the door itself seems to have been derived from woodwork (plate 102). Grotesque exaggeration of scale in ornament often appears in Seljuk work although this is an extreme example.

The Maristan is of the type of Nur ad-Din's at Damascus, but is here provided with a stone vaulted roof on columnar piers (plate 100). As in the mosque, the formerly open *sahn* is recalled by a fountain beneath an oculus.

The most typical of all Seljuk buildings are the fortified *hans*, or caravanserais, which line major trade routes a comfortable day's journey apart. The larger were royal foundations, such as the Sultan Han on the Konya-Aksaray Road, begun under Keykubad I in 1229 and completed seven years later (plate 103). The traveler entered the court by a single gate (plate 104). In the center stood a small mosque raised on vaults and approached by an outside stair. Surrounding the court were stone vaulted accommodations for guests, as well as a bath and quarters for

39

the attendants, who here included a band of musicians. The stables to the rear of the court had another monumental entrance and were lighted by a domed lantern.

The exterior portal of the Sultan Han presents the typical Seljuk interpretation of the *muqarnas* portal; really not a vault at all but half a corbeled dome. The pointed arch, prominent at Divrigi, has shrunk to a flat carved band. The frame, or *pishtaq*, which once rose as at Divrigi into a false front higher than the walls is so minutely carved that it recalls the tiled patterns of contemporary Persian architecture, upon which it was probably based. The joggled lintel, however, suggests a closer tie to the stone workers of Damascus, some of whom are known to have been active at Konya.

The Ince Minare, Madrasa of the Slender Minaret, at Konya was founded by the Vizir Fakreddin Sahip Ata in 1258 and completed from a design of the architect Keluk b. Abdullah in 1262. The building is a single-*iwan* madrasa attached behind the *qibla* wall of a mosque and minaret built earlier (plate 107).[21] The *sahn* is covered by a brick dome on triangular pendentives with an oculus, now covered by a modern lantern, over a square pool (plates 105, 106).[22] The portal's huge rectilinear knots, probably of Ayyubid inspiration, are frequent in thirteenth-century Damascene architecture, but the enormous inscription entwined around the door itself is unique (plate 108). The decorator of Qala'un's madrasa repeated the form some years later in plaster but, in characteristic Egyptian manner, with much greater restraint. The exuberance of the rich twisted forms of Seljuk ornament often suggests animal rather than plant forms, and animals indeed often appear, though usually defaced by later, more orthodox, generations. Central Asian shamanism and clan totems may be responsible. The same rich fantasy is characteristic of the portal sculpture of Gök Madrasa at Sivas, founded by the same patron in 1271 and signed by the same architect (plate 111). The use of paired minarets is Persian, but the cruciform plan—an open court with a pool surrounded by an arcade and *iwans* (plate 109)—would not be out of place in Damascus.

Hudavend, a daughter of Kiliçarslan IV (1246–64), must have been quite elderly when, in 1330, she was buried in her tomb, the Türbe of Hudavend Hatun, Nigde, already completed in 1312. Seljuk burial customs remained central Asian. Embalmed bodies were placed in vaults beneath the prayer chamber (plate 110). The stone roofs of these chambers might be domed but were more frequently pyramidal; and, although their immediate origin is the north Persian tomb towers of the eleventh century, they may ultimately be patterned after central Asian nomads' tents.[23] The structure has the overelaboration characteristic of a very late period of Seljuk style. *Muqarnas* "squinches" turn the octagonal plan into a sixteen-sided polygon, once intended to support a conical roof of as many facets (plate 112).[24]

THE OTTOMAN EMPIRE (1299–1922)

In the late thirteenth century the Ottoman Turks entered Anatolia as feudatories. With the collapse of the Seljuk dynasty their leader, Osman (1299–1326), declared himself Sultan, giving his name to his dynasty and his people. His successor, Orhan (1326–59), captured Prusa (Bursa) and made it his capital in the first year of his reign. Orhan's successor, Murad, moved the capital to Adrianople (Edirne) in 1366. Finally, Mehmet II (1451–81) captured Constantinople (Istanbul) in 1453. In the sixteenth and seventeenth centuries the Mediterranean became a virtually Turkish lake, and the ancient Arab empire was re-formed under the Turks with the addition of Greece, the Balkans, and Hungary. Of the vast revenue that the Empire poured into Constantinople, much was used for impressive building.

The Ulu Cami, or congregational mosque of Bursa, founded in the late fourteenth century, differed little from that of Divrigi except that its many identical bays were vaulted in brick rather than stone. The Seljuk madrasa was, however, also adapted as a mosque, constituting the first purely Ottoman architectural type. The finest example is the Yeşil Cami, or Green Mosque, founded by Mehmet I (1403–21), the main structure of which was finished in 1419, the ornament in 1424. Like its immediate predecessors, Yeşil Cami has loosely grouped around it a number of subsidiary structures (plate 114). These include a tomb, or *türbe*; a madrasa with an open *sahn*; and a *hamam*, or bath. Yeşil Cami faces a magnificent view of the city and, like all other mosques of this type, was intended to have an open portico, domically vaulted.

The *qibla iwan* and its two smaller companions have floors substantially higher than the "*sahn*" within which stands a fountain beneath a once-open oculus (plates 115, 116). The glory of the building lies in its magnificent tiles, predominantly blue-green, but occasionally polychromed and gilded. These were produced, according to an inscription on the *mihrab*, by artisans from the Persian city of Tabriz. Save for the marble east and west walls of the "sahn," all surfaces not encrusted with tile were covered with delicate painted ornament in black, ochre, and rose. The extreme elaboration and small scale of the pervasive ornamental patterns suggest that the original appearance was rather like the Hall of the Ambassadors in the Alhambra. Yeşil Cami impresses us as both the overrefined end of Seljuk art and the beginning of the new Ottoman style. The latter impression is strongest in the portal which, although it follows Seljuk tradition, has clarified and refined the forms (plate 113). For example, the *muqarnas* vault is no longer framed by an arch. The flowing arabesques of the spandrels will soon be dispensed with in later buildings.

A mosque-madrasa of the type of Yeşil Cami, however, could not be expanded to accommodate the large congregations produced by successive conquests. The well-known multi-columned type of Divrigi, followed by Bursa, while capable of indefinite expansion, was encumbered by heavy piers. There was, however, another pattern available in the south Anatolian mosques with their extensive open *sahns* and large domes, several bays square, over the *mihrabs*. These, derived ultimately from Damascus, looked, in plan, rather like that of Baybars in Cairo (plate 83). On this prototype, the Üç Şerefeli Mosque at Edirne was planned in 1438 and completed nine years later (plate 117).[25] The large dome resting on a hexagon reduces the need for interior supports, while to the Bursa portico have been added the arcades of a rectangular *sahn*. Domes of brick, lead-covered now rather than tiled as at Bursa, cover all the bays. The four minarets at the corners of the atrium, arranged in ascending order of height toward the prayer hall, are patterned in brick after the Seljuk manner but end in typically Ottoman pencil points (plate 118).

It is hard to imagine now the joyous burst of creative energy experienced by the Turkish nation upon the final conquest of Constantinople, now Istanbul. The hilly triangle of the ancient city commands breath-taking views over the Golden Horn, the Bosporus, and the Sea of Marmara; and the Ottomans had already shown, in Bursa, a strong sensitivity to the siting of their buildings. In 1463, ten years after the conquest, Mehmet II took the most commanding hill for his great Fatih Mosque. Completed in 1471, the original building was entirely rebuilt in the eighteenth century, save for the *sahn*; but the first plan (plate 119) is known to have followed that of the Üç Şerefeli at Edirne with the addition of a semidome over the *mihrab* bay.[26] Space was thus further increased without the addition of interior supports. The vast outer court, organizing the scattered dependent buildings of Yeşil Cami into a severely formal order, recalls the huge palace complexes of the Abbasids at Samarra, built when they too had controlled great revenues. Here, Mehmet endowed a whole university, every room with its lead-covered dome. Indeed, the city soon began to bubble with domes, as one imperial mosque after the other spread out its dependencies around it.

The next step was taken by the architect Heyruddin, who in 1501 began a mosque for Bayazid II, completed in 1506 (plates 121, 122). Heyruddin added another semidome to the plan of Fatih, so reproducing on a smaller scale the basic scheme of Justinian's Hagia Sophia of the sixth century. The similarity applies only to the vaults for, unlike the Byzantine models, supports are here so simplified as not to crowd the single rectangular prayer hall.[27] The portal of the *sahn* shows how much superfluous ornament the new and vigorous Ottoman style had pared away from the Seljuk forms it had inherited (plate 120). The square *sahn*, employing antique shafts with *muqarnas* capitals—the Ottoman "order" inherited from the Seljuks—is a little ponderous. However, its great height, enclosing a relatively small open area, engulfs the visitor in the shadow of its vaults, creating more sense of enclosure than any other *sahn* of its type (plate 123). It is probably this which has caused Bayazid's *sahn* to be especially extolled by visitors for its atmosphere of "peace, gravity, and reverence."

Rarely has an architectural style, entering upon the high moment of its development, so perfectly coincided with the lifetime of an architect of such genius as Koca Sinan (ca. 1490/91– 1588). Sinan, a Christian from Asia Minor, was brought to Constantinople in 1512 as a janissary. Beginning his army career in 1514, he served in Persia and Egypt as a military engineer and, in 1539, became Royal Architect. Living to a very ripe and active old age, he built scores of structures and planned hundreds more. He used the scheme of the Mosque of Bayazid II for his great Suleymaniye Mosque (plates 126, 127), 1549–57, but he also looked again at Hagia Sophia. He used the three conches opening from each semidome which Heyruddin had omitted, but, like Heyruddin, he cleared the space below them of all but a minimum of support. Then he set the "nave" arcades at the outer edges of the four great piers, reducing their arches to three (plate 125). In order to unify the space further, the tribunes were lowered and made structurally independent of the rest of the building. In so far as possible, the interior was kept a single unit to be perceived in its entirety at one view. The enormous size of the building is accentuated by the windows at floor level. Particularly in Turkish Islamic architecture, these have a fixed height, about that of a man, thus providing a scale from which the true size of any structure may instantly be read.

Sinan said of his own work that the Şehzade (plate 124) was the work of his apprenticeship, the Suleymaniye showed him to be a good workman, and the Mosque of Selim II at Edirne, begun in his eighty-fourth year, in 1569, was his masterpiece (plates 128, 130).[28] The Selimiye abandons the scheme of Hagia Sofia to raise its vast dome on an octagon of eight piers enclosed within a square. The dome, with a diameter of 103 feet, is still one of the largest in the world and the simplicity of the plan permitted an exterior structural harmony more effective than that of the Suleymaniye. The four very tall minarets, now at the corners of the prayer hall, have become for Edirne the architectural symbol provided for Seville by the Giralda. The great symmetrical mass, rising on a hill above its cluster of dependencies, which included a covered market (perhaps an allusion to the great trading center Edirne had become), may have been placed there, rather than in the capital, as a symbol of Ottoman imperial pretentions in Europe. It will be remembered that in little more than a hundred years the Turks were at the gates of Vienna.

The Mosque of Ahmet I, commonly called the Blue Mosque, or Ahmediye, was built by the Royal Architect, Mehmet Aga, between 1609 and 1616. Mehmet had been a pupil and coworker of Sinan's since 1566. To the scheme of the Suleymaniye he added two more semidomes (plate 129). The result, a radially symmetrical structure like the Selimiye, was not new to Ottoman architecture, having been tried on a smaller scale in Sinan's Şehzade Mosque of 1543–48 (plate 124). What is new is the superb monumentality of the exterior (plates 131, 132). From the gilded crescent at the apex of the great central cupola, a pyramidal mass of semidomes and subsidiary small domes cascades symmetrically toward the four lofty minarets at the corners of the prayer hall. Two lesser minarets at the corners of the atrium echo those of the Suleymaniye and make this structure a synthesis of all of its predecessors. In its exterior, the Ahmediye is perhaps the greatest achievement of Ottoman architecture. As has been said, no people have been more conscious of the siting of their buildings than the Ottomans, and here, beside the ancient hippodrome, was the most superb site in the world. Upon the furthermost promontory of Europe, the Ahmediye stands at the highest point. When one approaches the city by sea, the mosque appears faultlessly outlined high up against the sky. Its minarets move slowly across the convex pyramid they protect, and their gilded finials sparkle in the sun.

Turkish palaces of the fifteenth to the seventeenth century lacked the monumentality and even the symmetry of the great Imperial mosque complexes. Unlike the Abbasid palaces at Samarra or even the later Alhambra, they appear to have begun as relatively isolated pavilions set in enclosed gardens, perhaps reminiscent of the nomad tents of their ancestors. Only when it was necessary to house governmental functions were great courts added and, even then, the plan lacked strict axial symmetry. Of Mehmet the Conqueror's wooden palace on the site of the ancient Forum Tauri nothing now remains, but, probably as early as 1459, he began a new palace on the acropolis of the ancient city overlooking the Golden Horn and the Bosporus. This was later called Top Kapu Saray, or Cannon Gate Palace. The palace proper, which set the plan of the present building, was completed in 1465[29] and the outer enclosure by 1478/79 (plate 133). In the latter stands the Çinli Kiosk, or tile pavilion, begun, according to its inscription, in 1465 and finished in 1472. The plan is very like that of the central throne complex and *iwans* of the Bulkawara Palace and was probably transmitted to the Ottomans from Persia (plate 135). An extensive restoration of 1588 may be responsible for the awkward marble porch (plate 136). This does not seem to fit the articulation of the wall behind it whose divisions suggest there was once a more open structure, perhaps of wood. This would make the building look very like the seventeenth-century Safavid palaces of Isphahan.

Once in the new palace, Mehmet II and his successors progressively increased their imperial seclusion, holding audience while concealed behind a curtain as the Abbasid and Fatimid Caliphs and the Byzantine Emperors had once done. The forms Mehmet gave the Gate of Felicity and the Arz Odasi, or Throne Room, behind it are lost; but it is very probable they were both domed, as they still were in 1819 (plate 137). It remained the custom of the sultans down to the twentieth century to receive visitors on their coronations enthroned beneath the dome of the gate. Other audiences were held in the Arz Odasi behind it. The ceremonial association between monumental entrance and throne room has remained constant in Islam from Umayyad times almost until today. The ancient Oriental concepts of the public appearance and the enthronement of the autocrat beneath an astral symbol, the dome, to emphasize his semidivine status, have never quite died out.

Similarly, in all its forms and symbols, Islamic architecture has maintained an Eastern conservatism. We have noted the constant recurrence of the cruciform plan from Kufa to the Çinli Kiosk. Ornamental schemes are equally repetitive. The domed bedchamber of Murad III was added to the palace after a fire in 1574, probably from designs by Sinan (plate 134). Marble niches, similar to those in stucco at Samarra (compare plates 134 and 37), flank a wall fountain, while above them a magnificent inscription on a blue ground encircles the room, as does that of Abd al-Malik in the Dome of the Rock. Windows of pierced stucco, a technique already perfected at Khirbet al-Mafjar, occupy a wall of polychrome tile, continuing equally ancient principles of encrustation and of pattern repeated to infinity.

One cannot dismiss Seljuk architecture as a mere translation into stone of Persian wood and brick forms, although paired cylindrical minarets, *muqarnas* portals, the *pishtaq*, or false front, triangularly faceted pendentives, and other forms were all used earlier in Persia. Partly because stone replaces terra cotta, Seljuk ornament is apt to assume a much larger scale in relation to the walls to which it is applied; but there is in it a zoological element which is absent, or nearly so, in the rest of Islam. Even the abstract interlace often suggests, in Turkish hands, that somewhere in its background lurks a central Asian dragon. For all its busy surfaces, Seljuk architecture also maintains repose and balance, concentrating its ornament around portals and windows, leaving the walls between blank and smooth. It is an architecture of vaults in brick or stone, but its exterior appearance, except when an important dome was clothed with a pointed conical roof of stone, was rarely considered.

Ottoman architecture continues Seljuk traditions in its portals, in the use of smooth unadorned stone surfaces, and in its *muqarnas* capitals. But, in the conspicuous treatment given its domical vaults, it almost immediately breaks not only with the

46

Seljuk past but with that of Islam in general. There is no question about the fact that the original impetus for this evolution was given by the architecture of Byzantium whose heirs the Ottomans were and with which for so long they had maintained close contact. However, Byzantine experiments with vaulting systems —all based on Roman precedent—never seem to have lead them to the same conclusions reached by the Turks. After Hagia Sophia, Byzantine churches maintained a consistently small scale and their domes, set on very tall drums, achieved almost the effect of the bulbous Persian or even Egyptian Mamluk domes. The Ottomans returned to first principles and, beginning where Hagia Sophia had left off, carried Roman architecture through to a conclusion attained neither by the Romans nor by the Byzantines. As the vaults of the Imperial mosques grew larger, they increasingly dictated a correspondence between form and structure and between interior spaces and exterior design. In this, Ottoman architecture is unique in Islam and is comparable to French thirteenth-century Gothic, where such correspondence is also a dominant characteristic. Doubtless connected with the greater consciousness of external appearances is the close attention the Ottomans give to the choice of site. Elsewhere in Islam, it is rare to find the site intentionally chosen for its commanding position or its beautiful view.

CONCLUSION

Viewed as a whole, Islamic architecture, regardless of the program of a particular building, is God centered—as much as that of Gothic Europe. Mosques and palaces, although built for different purposes, created environments aloof from the outer world, predisposing their visitors toward contemplation. The complex ornament of a damascened tray, the intricate stucco patterns of the walls of a private house, or the endless arabesques of the tiled walls of a mosque invite, through their study, the submergence of the individual will into that of God. The formative years of Islamic architecture saw the perfecting of this quite specifically Eastern attitude toward the role of ornament in building and in life. Later Islamic architecture never lost this, but the temperaments of its patrons, which varied from country to country, imposed upon the architects new, and sometimes very different, interpretations.

North African, and particularly Spanish, Islamic architecture expresses an emotional fervor, a nervous energy, always characteristic of the Andalusian temperament. Cordoba's fantastic interlaced arches have an almost theatrical flamboyance. This quality is equally present in the Arabic poetry produced in such quantity in tenth-century Cordoba. An elegant sensuality appears in fourteenth-century Nazari literature and also in the architecture of the Court of Lions of the Alhambra.

Egypt, on the other hand, imposes a rather dry, precise logic on its buildings. It is probably not a coincidence that the paramount Muslim university in the world, al-Azhar, was founded in Cairo. The formality and measure imposed by custom upon living habits is expressed in the ceremonial elaboration of the dwelling and the precise spatial order of the cruciform madrasa.

Perhaps an inheritance from their pre-Muslim shamanism predisposed both the Seljuk and the Ottoman Turks toward mysticism. As a result, the Ottoman masterpieces, the great Imperial mosques, add a new element to Islamic architecture, the symbolic use of light, both natural and artificial, as a mystical synonym for God. Surah 24 of the Koran reads, in part, "God is the light of the Heavens and the earth. His light is as a niche in which is a lamp and the lamp is in a glass, the glass is as though it were a glittering star." Representations of a niche with a lamp suspended in it are frequent. They appear in stone on the façade of the Mosque of al-Aqmar in Cairo, often in glass windows, and in polychrome tile in the *mihrab* of the *türbe* of Mehmet I at Bursa. They were also a favorite motif in Turkish prayer rugs. One is reminded of the begging bowl or the stupa substituted for images of the Buddha at Sanchi. The single vast hollowed space which is the interior of any one of the great mosques of Constantinople or of Edirne can be likened to an enormous niche. By day, innumerable colored glass windows fill it with light. By night, glass lamps hanging not far above one's head provided, before they were electrified, a haze of soft, glowing light from innumerable burning wicks floating in oil. During the month of daytime fasting called Ramadan, the mosques are lighted all night, so that the glow on each hill is like so many enormous lanterns. Truly they are glittering stars testifying to the immediate and universal presence of God.

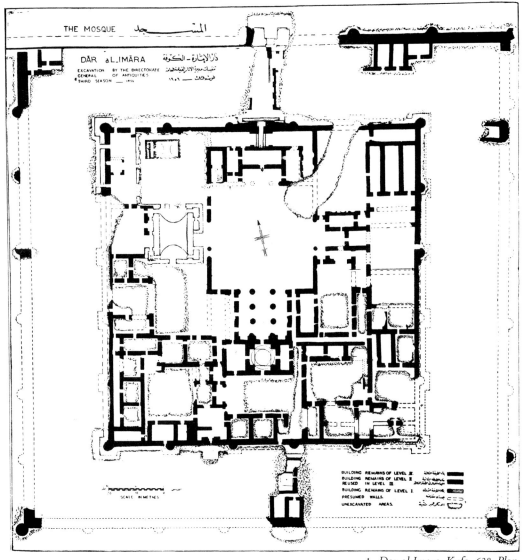

THE MOSQUE المسجد

DĀR aL.IMĀRA دارالإمارة ـ الكوفة

EXCAVATION BY THE DIRECTORATE
GENERAL OF ANTIQUITIES
THIRD SEASON ___ 1956

تنقيبات مديرية الآثار القديمة العامة
الموسم الثالث ___ ١٩٥٦

SCALE IN METRES

BUILDING REMAINS OF LEVEL Ⅳ
BUILDING REMAINS OF LEVEL Ⅱ
REUSED IN LEVEL Ⅲ
BUILDING REMAINS OF LEVEL I
PRESUMED WALLS
UNEXCAVATED AREAS

1. Dar al-Imara, Kufa, 638. Plan.

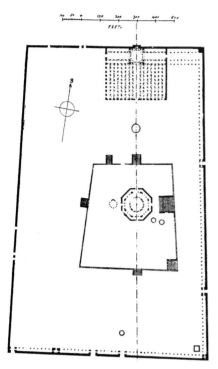

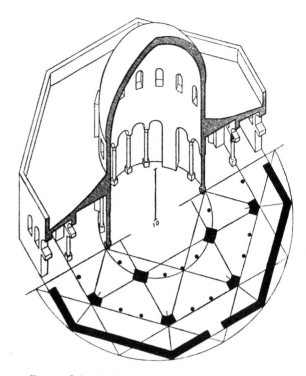

2. *Haram as Sharif, Jerusalem.*
   Plan, in the tenth century.

3. *Dome of the Rock. Diagram showing*
   geometric order of the plan.

4. *Dome of the Rock, Jerusalem, 688/89–691/92. Temple area seen from above (in background, Mosque*
   of al-Aqsa).

5. Dome of the Rock. Interior, ambulatory.

6. Dome of the Rock. Interior, the sakhra.

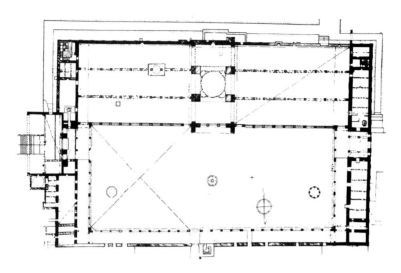

7. *Great Mosque of Damascus, 706–714/15. Plan. (Credit: Creswell)*

8. *Great Mosque of Damascus. Bab al-Barid, west entrance from sahn.*

9. *Great Mosque of Damascus. West side of sahn. (Photo: Creswell)*

10. *Great Mosque of Damascus. Façade of sanctuary. (Photo: Creswell)*

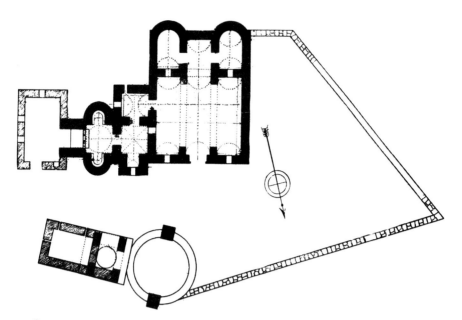

11. Qusayr Amra, ca. 715. Plan of the baths.

12. Qusayr Amra. Exterior of the baths. (Photo: Creswell)

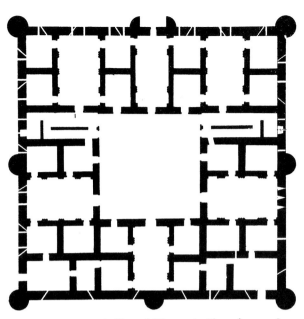

13. Qasr al-Kharanah. Plan of upper floor.

14. Qasr al-Kharanah, Transjordan, before 711. Entrance façade.

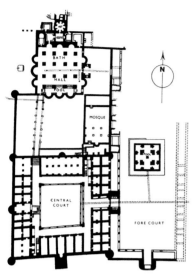

15. *Khirbet al-Mafjar, Jordan Valley, ca. 743–44. Plan.*

16. *Khirbet al-Mafjar. Mosaic floor of Audience Chamber in the bath.*

SCALE 2 0 1 2 3 4 5   10   15   20   25   30 METRES

17. Khirbet al-Mafjar. Façade of mansion, restored.

18. Khirbet al-Mafjar. Interior of
Audience Chamber of bath.

19. Khirbet al-Mafjar. Porch of the
bath entrance, restored.

20. *Mshatta. Detail of south façade. (Photo: Creswell)*

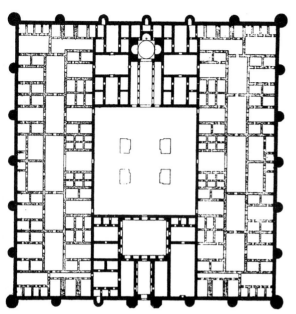

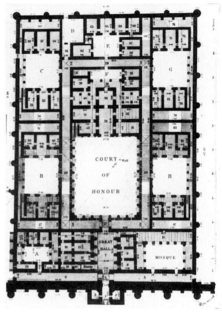

21. *Mshatta, Syria, ca. 750. Plan.*

22. *Ukhaidir, near Baghdad, ca. 774/775. Plan of central structure. (Credit: Creswell)*

23. *Ukhaidir, south façade of Court of Honor and boundary wall.*

24. *Ukhaidir. Great entrance hall looking north. (Photo: Creswell)*

25. *Ukhaidir. North façade of Court of Honor, present state. (Photo: Creswell)*

26. Ukhaidir. Dome in entrance passage. (Photo: Creswell)

27. Ukhaidir. North façade of Court of Honor, restored.

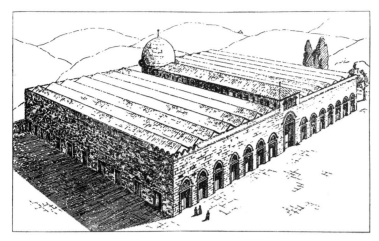

28. Mosque of al-Aqsa, Jerusalem. *Restored view of exterior as rebuilt by the Caliph al-Mahdi in 780. (Credit: Creswell)*

29. *Mosque of al-Aqsa.* Mihrab *aisle.*

30. *Great Mosque of Qairawan.* Mihrab *bay. (Photo: Creswell*

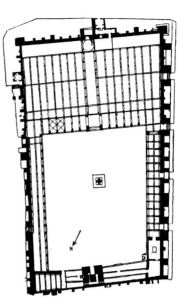

31. *Great Mosque of Qairawan. View of dome over* mihrab. *(Photo: Creswell)*

32. *Great Mosque of Qairawan. Pla*

33. *Great Mosque of Qairawan, 836–62. General view from the north. (Photo: Creswell)*

34. Jausaq al-Kharqani, Samarra. 836. Bab al-Amma.

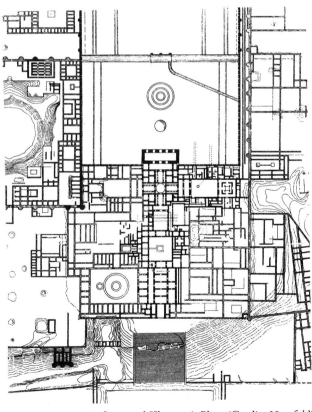

35. Jausaq al-Kharqani, Plan. (Credit: Herzfeld)

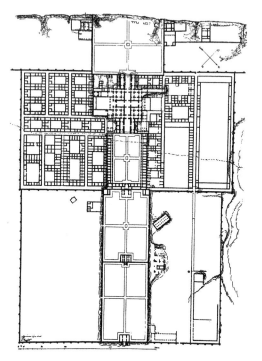

36. *Bulkawara Palace, Samarra, 849–59. Plan.*

37. *Bulkawara Palace. Stucco ornament in hall.*

38. Great Mosque of Samarra, begun 847. Minaret and exterior wall.

39. The Baghdad Gate of Raqqa, 772. (Photo: Creswell)

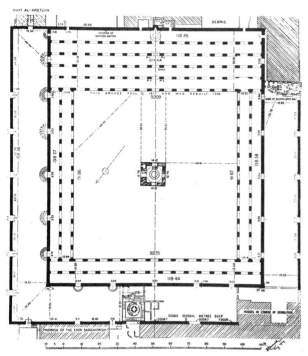

40. Mosque of Ibn Tulun, Cairo, finished 879. Plan. (Credit: Creswell)

41. Mosque of Ibn Tulun. General view. (Photo: Creswell)

42. Mosque of Ibn Tulun. Interior, restored. (Photo: Creswell)

43. Mosque of Ibn Tulun. View of inner arcades before restoration.

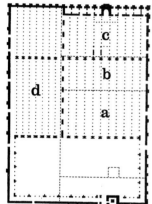

44. *Mosque of Cordoba, 785–987.*
Plan in the tenth century.
(a) Mosque of Abd
er-Rahman I; (b) Addition
of Abd er-Rahman II;
(c) Addition of Hakam II;
(d) Addition of al-Mansur.

45. *Mosque of Cordoba. Interior, work of Abd er-Rahman I,* 785.

46. *Mosque of Cordoba. East façade, begun 987, view before restoration.*

47. *Mosque of Cordoba. The lantern, chapel of Villaviciosa, 961–68.*

49. Mosque of Cordoba. Vault of bay to right of mihrab.

50. Mosque of Cordoba. Vault over mihrab bay, 961–68.

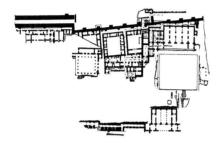

51. *Palace at Medina az-Zahra, 936–76. Plan of partially excavated palace.*

52. *Palace at Medina az-Zahra. Hall of Abd er-rahman II. Detail of door jamb.*

53. *Palace at Medina az-Zahra. Hall of Abd er-rahman II, completed 957.*

54. Mosque of Qarawiyin, Fez, 1135–43. Vault of mihrab aisle.

55. *Mosque of Tlemcen, 1136. Vault over the* mihrab *bay.*

56. *Mosque of Tlemcen. Mihrab bay.*

57. *Mosque of Tinmal, 1153. Qibla aisle.*

59. Kutubiyya Mosque, Marrakesh, ca. 1150. Transverse view.

58. Mosque of Tinmal. Mihrab.

60. Mosque of Seville, 1172–76. Sahn.

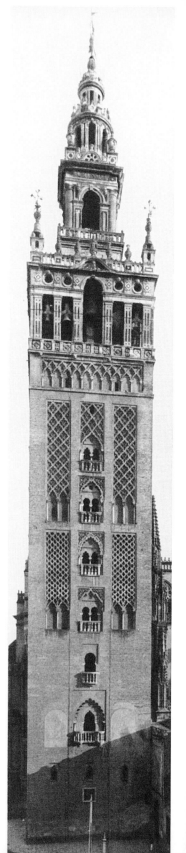

61. Mosque of Seville. Minaret (Giralda Tower), finished 1195.

62. Mosque at Taza, 1291–92. Mihrab vault.

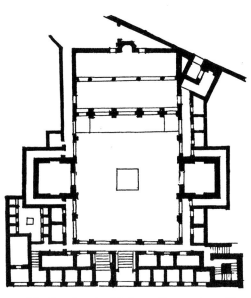

63. The Bou Inaniya Madrasa, Fez, 1350–55. Plan.

64. The Bou Inaniya Madrasa. Sahn.

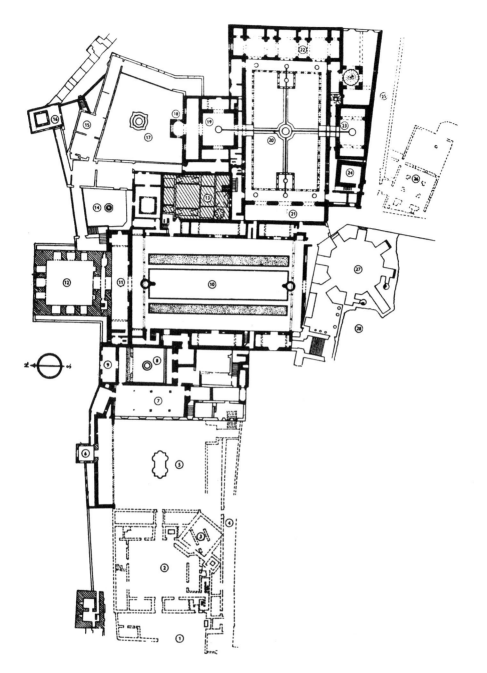

65. The Alhambra Palace, Granada. Plan. (1) Original entrance; (2) First court; (3) Mosque; (4) Road;
(5) Court of Machuco; (6) Tower of Machuco; (7) Mexuar; (8) Court of the Cuarto Dorado; (9) Cuarto
Dorado; (10) Court of Myrtles, or Alberca; (11) Chamber of la Barca; (12) Hall of the Ambassadors;
(13) Bath; (14) Court of the Screen; (15) Quarters of Charles V; (16) Tower of the Queen's Boudoir;
(17) Garden of Daraxa; (18) Mirader of Daraxa; (19) Chamber of the Two Sisters; (20) Court of Lions;
(21) Hall of the Mocárabes; (22) Hall of Justice; (23) Hall of the Abencerages; (24) Cistern; (25) Ditch;
(26) Tomb; (27 and 28) Palace of Charles V, begun 1526.

66. The Alhambra. Hall of the Ambassadors, 1333–54.

67. The Alhambra. Court of Lions toward the east.

68. The Alhambra. The Hall of the Abencerages, ceiling.

69. *The Alhambra. Hall of Justice, 1354–91.*

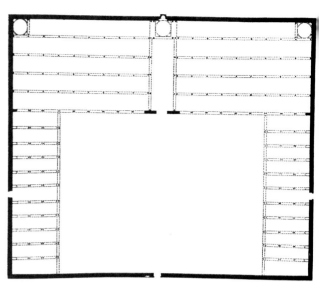

70. *Mosque of Mahdiya, ca. 912/13. North portal. (Photo: Creswell)*

71. *Mosque of al-Azhar, Cairo, 970. Restored plan. (Credit: Creswell)*

72. *Mosque of al-Azhar. Sahn, 1130-49 (before restorations of 1892).*

73. *Mosque of al-Azhar. Mihrab aisle. (Photo: Creswell)*

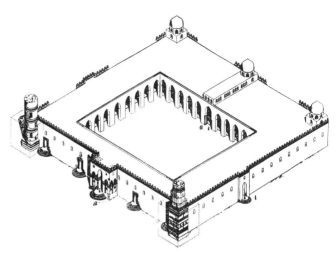

74. *Mosque of al-Hakim, Cairo, 990–1013. Reconstruction. (Credit: Creswell)*

75. *Mosque of al-Hakim. Detail of the north portal, 1103–13. (Photo: Creswell)*

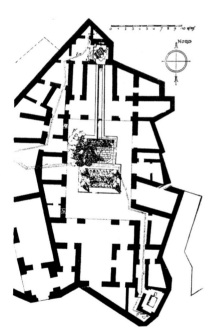

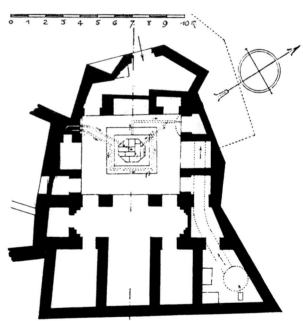

76. House at al-Fustat, near Cairo,
    first half of the eleventh century.
    Plan. (Credit: Creswell)

77. House at al-Fustat, first half of the eleventh century.
    Plan. (Credit: Creswell)

78. *Bab al-Futuh, Cairo, 1087. Longitudinal elevation. (Credit: Creswell)*

79. *Bab al-Futuh. (Photo: Creswell)*

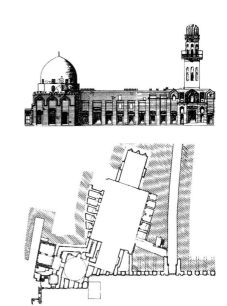

80. Madrasa of Sultan Salih Negm ad-Din, Cairo, 1242–43/44. Elevation and plan. (Credit: Creswell)

81. Mosque of al-Aqmar, Cairo, finished 1125. Façade. (Photo: Creswell)

82. Mosque of Sultan Baybars.
Façade. (Photo: Creswell)

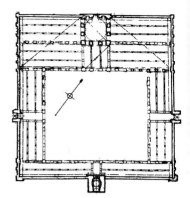

83. Mosque of Sultan Baybars, Cairo, 1267–69.
Restored plan. (Credit: Creswell)

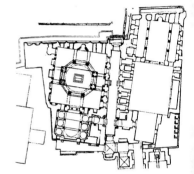

85. Madrasa and Tomb of Sultan
Qala'un. Plan. (Credit: Creswell)

84. Madrasa and Tomb of Sultan Qala'un, Cairo, 1284–85. Façade. (Photo: Creswell)

86. Tomb of Sultan Qala'un. Interior. (Photo: Creswell)

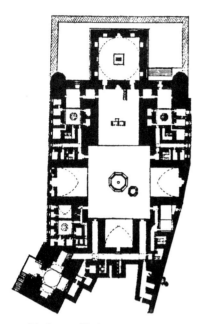

87. Madrasa of Sultan Hasan, Cairo,
1356–62/63. Plan.

88. Madrasa of Sultan Hasan. Sahn.

89. Madrasa of Sultan Hasan. Portal.

90. *Madrasa and Tomb of Sultan Qayt Bay, Cairo, 1472–74. Exterior.*

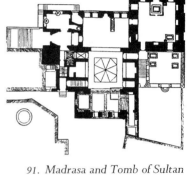

91. *Madrasa and Tomb of Sultan Qayt Bay. Plan.*

92. *Madrasa and Tomb of Sultan Qayt Bay. Sahn.*

93. *House of Gamal ad-Din az-Zahabi, Cairo, 1637. Hosh and* maqad.

94. *House of Gamal ad-Din az-Zahabi. Qa'a.*

95. *Madrasa and Tomb of Qani Bay Akhur, Cairo, 1503.*

96. *Maristan of Nur ad-Din, Damascus, begun 1154. Vault of antechamber.*

97. *Maristan of Nur ad-Din. Portal.*

98. *Maristan of Nur ad-Din. Plan.*

99. *Madrasa of Nur ad-Din, Damascus, 1172. Plan.*

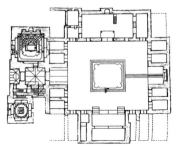

100. Ulu Cami, Divrigi, begun 1228/29. Interior of Maristan.

101. Ulu Cami and Maristan. Plan and section.

102. Ulu Cami. North portal.

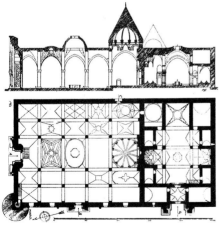

103. Sultan Han, near Konya, 1229–36. Plan.

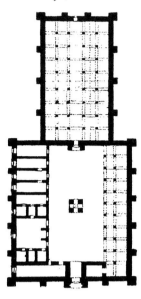

104. Sultan Han. Exterior portal.

105. Ince Minare, Konya, 1258–62. General exterior.

106. Ince Minare. Interior of dome.

107. Ince Minare. Plan.

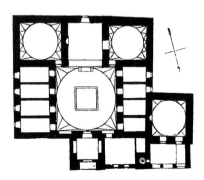

108. Ince Minare. Portal.

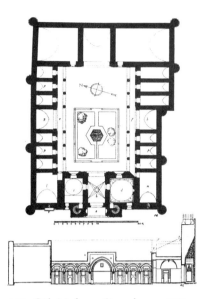

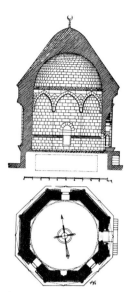

109. Gök Madrasa, Sivas, begun 1271.
Plan and section, restored.

110. Tomb of Hudavend Hatun, Nigde,
finished 1312. Plan and section.

111. Gök Madrasa. Entrance façade.

112. Tomb of Hudavend Hatun.

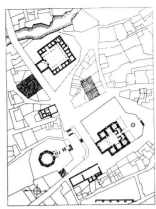

114. *Yeşil Cami. General site plan including surroundings.*

113. *Yeşil Cami, Bursa, finished 1419. Portal.*

115. *Yeşil Cami. Interior looking north.*   116. *Yeşil Cami. Longitudinal section.*

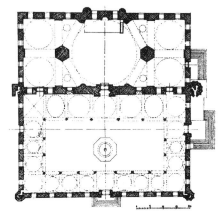

117. Mosque of Üç Şerefeli, Edirne, 1438–47. Plan.

118. Mosque of Üç Şerefeli. General exterior.

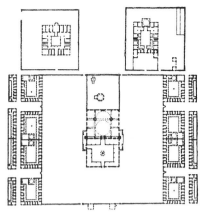

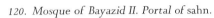

119. *Mosque of Fatih, Istanbul, 1471. Plan of complex, mosque restored to original state.*

120. *Mosque of Bayazid II. Portal of sahn.*

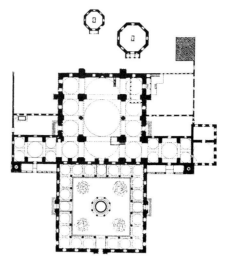

121. Mosque of Bayazid II, Istanbul, 1501–06. Plan.

122. Mosque of Bayazid II. Exterior.

123. *Mosque of Bayazid II.* Sahn.

124. Şehzade Mosque, Istanbul, 1543–48. General exterior.

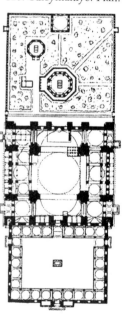

125. Suleymaniye, Istanbul, 1549–57. Interior.

127. Suleymaniye. General exterior

128. Selimiye, Edirne, 1569–75. Plan.   *129. Mosque of Ahmet I (Blue Mosque), Istanbul, 1609–16. Plan.*

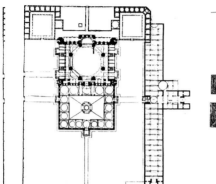
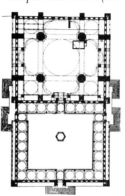

130. The Selimiye. General exterior.   *131. Mosque of Ahmet I. Exterior.*

132. Mosque of Ahmet I. Exterior.

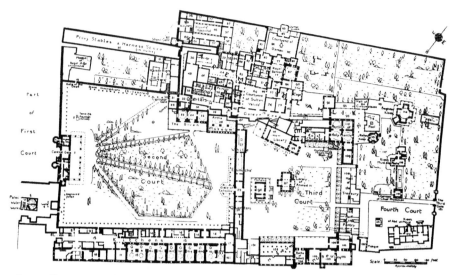

133. Top Kapu Saray, Constantinople, begun ca. 1459. Plan.

134. Top Kapu Saray. Bedchamber of Murad III, soon after 1574.

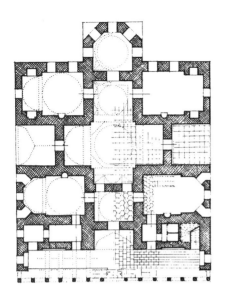

135. *Top Kapu Saray. Çinli Kiosk, 1465–72. Plan.*

136. *Top Kapu Saray. Çinli Kiosk. Exterior.*

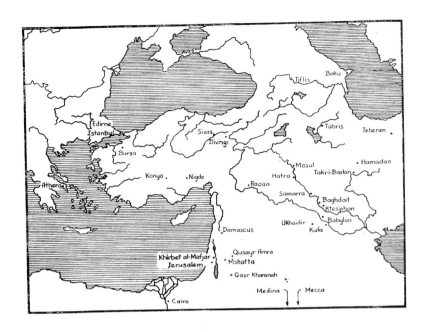

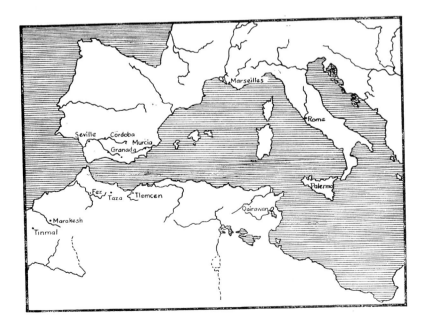

113

NOTES

1. *Koran, The,* E. H. Palmer, trans. (Oxford University Press, 1947), is used throughout this essay whenever *The Koran* is quoted.

2. Quoted by K. A. C. Creswell, *A Short Account of Early Muslim Architecture,* Penguin Books, 1958, p. 4.

3. *Encyclopedia of Islam,* Vol. IV, pp. 29–30.

4. Very few survive, but the enclosure around the cenotaph of Sultan Qala'un in Cairo gives an idea of how they must have looked (plate 86).

5. Oleg Grabar, "The Umayyad Dome of the Rock in Jerusalem," *Ars Orientalis,* Vol. III, 1959.

6. *Ibid.*

7. R. W. Hamilton in his *Khirbet al-Mafjar* (Oxford, 1959, pp.

343 f.) has suggested that the owner may have been Walid ibn al-Yazd, poet and pleasure lover, who became Caliph in 743–44 and was assassinated the same year.

8. See Irwing Lavin, "The House of the Lord: Aspects of the Role of Palace Triclinia in the Architecture of Late Antiquity and the Early Middle Ages," *Art Bulletin*, XLIV, March, 1962, pp. 1–27.

9. See Oleg Grabar's discussion in *The World of Islam, Studies in Honor of Philip K. Hitti*, London, 1959, pp. 99 ff.

10. K. A. C. Creswell, *Early Muslim Architecture*, Vol. II, Oxford, Clarendon Press, 1940, pp. 94 ff.

11. This holds true even for Sicily and Spain where, in the twelfth and fourteenth centuries respectively, structures purely Islamic except for minor decorative details were erected for Christian patrons.

12. The belfry and the three-tiered cupola above it were added in the sixteenth century.

13. As quoted by K. A. C. Creswell, *The Muslim Architecture of Egypt*, Vol. I, Oxford, Clarendon Press, 1952, p. 33.

14. The origins were discussed in Chapter II, p. 24.

15. Creswell in *The Muslim Architecture of Egypt* (Vol. I, p. 99) cites the Qa'at ad-Dardir as the earliest surviving example. The "*iwans*" were vaulted in brick, while the higher central lantern had a wooden roof.

16. Creswell (*ibid.*, p. 201) finds the closest parallels in the twelfth-century architecture of Norman Sicily.

17. This type of portal is related to the half dome over a square niche in the great hall at Ukhaidir (plate 24). The half dome recurs at the Bab al-Amma of Samarra (plate 34) supported by squinches. In the Maristan of Nur ad-Din at Damascus of 1154 (plate 96) the squinches have so multiplied into *muqarnas* that there is not much of the half dome left. The form was first introduced into Egypt from Syria in Baybars' madrasa of 1262–63.

18. Ever since the late thirteenth century, horseshoe arches both round and pointed, types of corbels, and patterns in stucco ornament suggest the presence of Moorish craftsmen in

Cairo; they were probably Spaniards fleeing the Christian conquest of their country.

19. The pediment appears to be a re-used fragment, probably of late Roman date. For the history of the semidome portal see note 17.

20. A list is given by Tamara Talbot Rice, *The Seljuks in Asia Minor*, London, 1961, pp. 196–205.

21. Behcet Ünsal, *Turkish Islamic Architecture*, London, 1959, p. 34.

22. According to Tamara Talbot Rice (*op. cit.*, p. 138), such pendentives, characteristic of Seljuk and Ottoman architecture, were first used in the Chidsa Rabi near Meshed in 1026.

23. *Ibid.*, p. 41.

24. It is a strange coincidence to find the same projecting "squinches" of *muqarnas* used not many years later in the Alhambra (plate 68).

25. A *şerefe* is the balcony of a minaret. This is the first time a minaret was built with three, hence Üç Şerefeli.

26. Behcet Ünsal, *op. cit.*, p. 24.

27. The same desire for uninterrupted floor space appears when the columns supporting the center domes of several of the smaller Byzantine churches of the city were, about this time, replaced by arches reaching almost to the outer walls.

28. Celal Esad Arseven, *L'Art Turc*, Istanbul, 1939, p. 167.

29. Barnette Miller, *Beyond the Sublime Porte*, New Haven, 1931, p. 35.

GLOSSARY

badiya	— a semipermanent camp, generally used as a hunting lodge
bayt	— an Arabic term for house, frequently used to designate the self-contained apartments into which Omayyad mansions and Abbasid palaces are divided
durqa	— a square, depressed central space in the main area of a medieval Cairo house
faradis	— a walled-in place, or garden (Persian source of the word "paradise")
hajj	— the pilgrimage which all Muslims should make to Mecca once during their lives
hamam	— a bath, public or private
han	— an Arabic term for fortified buildings along trade routes furnishing accommodations for

merchants, their goods, and travelers. (the Persian equivalent is caravanserai)

hosh	— the inner court of an Egyptian house
iwan	— an open porch, recessed from a court, often used to indicate the raised chambers opening off a domestic covered central area
madrasa	— a theological school, originally Persian
maqad	— an open loggia, opening off the *hosh* in an Egyptian house
maqsura	— a protective partition of wood or brick surrounding the *minbar* and *mihrab*
maristan	— the Persian word for hospital
maydan	— an open, central space
mihrab	— a niche in the *qibla* wall of a mosque, indicating the direction of Mecca
minbar	— a pulpit from which the Friday prayer is spoken
muqarnas	— Arabic term for a stalactite vault, see page 24
mushrabiyya	— a kind of interlaced wooden screenwork, used to cover the street-facing windows in an Egyptian house
pishtaq	— a square, raised frame surrounding the entrance arch of an important Muslim building
qa'a	— a ceremonial reception hall in an Egyptian house
qibla wall	— that wall of a mosque which faces Mecca
riwaq	— an arcade surrounding the *sahn*
sabil	— a public drinking fountain
sahn	— an interior court (usually in a mosque)
sakhra	— the bare rock surface of the summit of Mount Moriah, traditionally the site of the altar on which Abraham sacrificed Isaac
şerefe	— a Turkish term for the balcony of a minaret
türbe	— a Turkish term for the building over a tomb
ziyadah	— the outer court of a mosque

BIBLIOGRAPHY

Ars Orientalis, Vol. III. Ann Arbor, University of Michigan, 1959.

Arseven, Celal Esad, *L'Art Turc*. Istanbul, Devlet Basimevi, 1939.

Briggs, M. S., *Muhammadan Architecture in Egypt and Palestine*. Oxford, Clarendon Press, 1924.

Brockelmann, Carl, *History of the Islamic Peoples*, trans. by Joel Carmichael and Moshe Perlmann. New York, Capricorn Books, 1960.

Creswell, K. A. C., *Early Muslim Architecture*, 2 vols. Oxford, Clarendon Press, 1932–40.

——, *The Muslim Architecture of Egypt*, 2 vols. Oxford, Clarendon Press, 1952–59.

——, *A Short Account of Early Muslim Architecture*. Baltimore, Penguin, 1958.

Diez, E., and Gluck, H., *Die Kunst der Islam*, Propyläon Kunstgeschichte V. Berlin, Propyläon Verlag, 1925.

Egli, Ernst, *Sinan, Der Baumeister Osmanischer Glanzzeit*. Stuttgart, Erlanbach-Zürich Verlag, 1954.

Gabriel, Albert, *Une Capitale Turque, Brousse, Bursa*, 2 vols. Paris, Editions de Boccard, 1958.

——, *Monuments Turcs d'Anatolie*, 2 vols. Paris, Editions de Boccard, 1934.

Gomez-Moreno, Manuel, *Ars Hispaniae* ("El Arte Arabe Español"), Vol. III. Madrid, Editorial Plus Ultra, 1951.

Gurlit, C., *Die Baukunst Konstantinopels*, 3 vols. Berlin, Wasmuth, 1912.

Hamilton, R. W., *Khirbet al Mafjar*. Oxford, Clarendon Press, 1959.

——, *The Structural History of the Aqsa Mosque*. London, Oxford University Press, 1949.

Herzfeld, E., *Ars Islamica* ("Damascus, Studies in Architecture"), Vol. IX (1942), pp. 1–53; Vol. X (1943), pp. 13–70; Vols. XI-XII (1946), pp. 1–71. Ann Arbor, University of Michigan Press.

——, *Erste vorläufiger Bericht über die Ausgrabungen von Samarra*. Berlin, 1912.

——, *Geschichte der Stadt Samarra*. Hamburg, Eckardt & Messtorff (n.d.).

Hitti, Philip K., *History of the Arabs*, 6th ed. London, Macmillan; New York, St. Martin's Press, 1937.

——, *The World of Islam*, ed. by James Kritzeck and R. Bayly Winder. London, Macmillan; New York, St. Martin's Press, 1959.

Jaussen and Savignac, *Mission Archéologique en Arabie*, Vol. III. Paris, Paul Geuthner, 1922.

Koran, The, trans. by E. H. Palmer. London, Oxford University Press, 1947.

Lankaster, Harding, *The Antiquities of Jordan*. New York, 1959.

Mamboury, Ernest, *Constantinople*. Constantinople, Rizzo and Son, 1925.

Marcais, Georges, *L'Architecture Musulmane d'Occident.* Paris, Arts et Métiers Graphiques, 1954.

Miller, Barnette, *Beyond the Sublime Porte.* New Haven, Yale University Press, 1931.

Mustafa, Mohammed Ali, *Sumer: A Journal of Archaeology in Iraq* ("Dar al Imara at Kufa"), Vol. XIII. Baghdad-Iraq, The Directorate General of Antiquities, 1947. Also, Vols. X (1954) and XII (1956).

Reuther, O., *Ocheidir Wissenschaftliche Veroffentlichung der Deutschen Orient Gesellschaft*, No. 20. Leipzig, 1912.

Rice, Tamara Talbot, *The Seljuks in Asia Minor.* London, Thames and Hudson, 1961.

Richmond, E. T., *Moslem Architecture.* London, Royal Asiatic Society, 1926.

Terrasse, Henri, *Ars Orientalis* ("La Mosque d'al-Qarawiyin à Fez et l'art des Almorovides"), Vol. II. Washington, D.C., Smithsonian Publication No. 4298, 1957.

Torres Balbás, Leopoldo, *Ars Hispaniae* ("Arte Almohade," "Arte Nazarí," "Arte Mudéjar"), Vol. IV. Madrid, Editorial Plus Ultra, 1949.

——, *Artes Almoravide y Almohade*, Series Artes y Artistas. Madrid, Instituto Diego Velasquez de Consejo Superior de Investigaciones Científicas, 1955.

——, *La Mezquita de Cordoba y las ruinas de Madinat al-Zahra*, Los Monumentos Cardinales de España, Vol. XIII. Madrid, Editorial Plus Ultra, (n.d.).

Ünsal, Behcet, *Turkish Islamic Architecture.* London, Tiranti, 1959.

INDEX

Numbers in regular roman type refer to text pages; *italic* figures refer to the plates.

SOURCES OF ILLUSTRATIONS

Alinari-Anderson, Florence: 61, 66

American Colony Photos, Jerusalem; (photo by S. Mck. Crosby): 5, 6

Arab Information Center, New York: 4, 8, 23, 38

Arseven, C. E. L'Art Turc (Istanbul, 1939): 103, 107

Bonfils, Cairo: 43

Briggs, M. S., Muhammadan Architecture in Egypt and Palestine, Clarendon Press (Oxford, 1924): 87

Byne, Arthur,: 49, 67

Choisy, A., Histoire de l'Architecture (Paris, 1929): 3

Creswell, K. A. C., Early Muslim Architecture, Vol. I, Clarendon Press (Oxford, 1932): 7, 9, 10, 12, 20; (Vol. II, 1940): 22, 24, 25, 26, 28, 30, 31, 33, 35, 39, 40, 41, 42

Creswell, K. A. C., The Muslim Architecture of Egypt, Vol. I, Clarendon Press (Oxford, 1952): 70, 71, 73, 74, 75, 76, 77, 78, 79, 81; (Vol. II, 1959): 80, 82, 83, 84, 85, 86

Diez, E. and Gluck H., Der Kunst der Islam, Propyläon Kunstgeschichte V, (Berlin, 1925): Maps (redrawn), 21, 32, 91, 126

Foto Mas, Barcelona: 45, 47, 48, 50, 52, 53, 56, 60

Foto Marburg, Marburg-Lahn: 93, 94

Gabriel, Albert, Monuments Turcs d'Anatolie, Editions de Boccard (Paris, 1934): 100, 101, 102, 109, 110, 111, 112

Gabriel, Albert, Une Capitale Turque, Brousse, Bursa, Editions de Boccard (Paris, 1958): 114, 116

Gurlit, C., Die Baukunst Konstantinopels, Ernst Wasmuth Verlag (Berlin, 1912): 121, 128, 129

Hamilton, R. W., Khirbet al Mafjar, Clarendon Press (Oxford, 1959): 17, 18, 19

Courtesy of the Herzfeld Archives, Freer Gallery of Art, Smithsonian Institution, Washington, D.C.: 96

Herzfeld, E., "Damascus, Studies in Architecture," Ars Islamica, IX, Part I, 1942: 97, 99; Ars Islamica, XI-XII, 1946: 98

Herzfeld, E., Erste Vorläufiger Bericht über die Ausgrabungen von Samarra, Dietrich Reimer Verlag (Berlin, 1912): 36

Iraq Museum, Baghdad: 1

Jaussen and Savignac, Mission Archéologique en Arabie, Vol. III (Paris, 1922): 11, 13, 14

Lankaster, Harding, The Antiquities of Jordan, Lutterworth Press (London, 1959): 15

Lekegian, G., Cairo: 72, 88, 89, 90, 92, 95

Majewski, Lawrence, New York: 29, 105, 113, 122, 123, 124

Marcais, G., L'Architecture Musulmane d'Occident, Arts et Métiers Graphiques (Paris, 1954): 44, 63

Melling, Voyage Pittoresque du Constantinople et des rives du Bosphore (Paris, 1819): 137

Palestine Archaeological Museum, Jerusalem: 16

Penzer, N. M., The Harem, G. Harrap & Company Limited, (London, 1936): 133

Powell, Josephine, Rome: 115, 125, 127, 132, 136

Reuther, O., Ocheidir Wissenschaftliche Veroffentlichung der Deutschen Orient Gesellschaft (Leipzig, 1912): 27

Richmond, E. T., Moslem Architecture, Royal Asiatic Society (London, 1926): 2

Seligmann-Chapelle: 57

Staatliche Museen zu Berlin: 34, 37

Terrasse, Henri, Madrid: 58, 59, 62

Terrasse, Henri, "La Mosque d'al-Qarawiyin à Fez et l'art des Almorovides, "Ars Orientalis, II, 1957: 54

Torres Balbás, Leopoldo, "Arte Almohade," "Arte Nazari," "Arte Mudéjar," Ars Hispaniae, IV (Madrid, 1949): 65

—— La Mezquita de Cordoba y las ruinas de Madinat Al-Zahra, Los Monumentos Cardinales de Espana, XIII (Madrid, n.d.): 51

Turkish Government: 104, 130

Turkish Information Office, New York: 108, 131

Ünsal, Behcet, *Turkish Islamic Architecture*, Alec Tiranti Ltd. (London, 1959): 106, 117, 118, 119, 120, 135

Vernacci, J. Ruiz, Madrid: 68

Courtesy of Yale University, School of Fine Arts, New Haven, Connecticut: 46, 64, 69, 134

Printed in photogravure and letterpress by Joh. Enschedé en Zonen, Haarlem, The Netherlands. Set in Romulus with Spectrum display, both faces designed by Jan van Krimpen. Format by William and Caroline Harris.